Mingled Voices 2
International Proverse Poetry Prize Anthology 2017
Proverse Hong Kong
2018

MINGLED VOICES 2 is an anthology of eighty-nine poems, the work of sixty-one poets, selected from those which were entered in the second annual international competition for the Proverse Poetry Prize in 2017.

The Proverse Poetry Prize was jointly founded in 2016 by Dr Gillian Bickley and Dr Verner Bickley MBE, in association with the annual international Proverse Prize for unpublished book-length fiction, non-fiction or poetry, submitted in English, which they also founded, in 2008.

Poems could be submitted on any subject or topic chosen by each poet or on the subject chosen for 2017 by the Administrators, "Happiness". There was a free choice of form and style.

Included in the anthology are the poems that won the first, second, and third prizes. Selection to appear in the anthology was also awarded by the judges for the Prize.

The places of birth of the writers whose work is included in the anthology range from Scandinavia to the Far East, to the southern hemisphere; and include Australia, Bulgaria, Canada, Cuba, Denmark, Estonia, Georgia, Hong Kong, Hungary, India, Italy, Macedonia, Macau, New Zealand, the People's Republic of China, Poland, South Africa, Spain, Turkey, the UK and the USA. Some have strong links with other countries, including East Germany and Zambia.

Mingled Voices 2
International Proverse Poetry Prize Anthology 2017

Contributors

Abbie Taylor, Allegra Silberstein, Angelo Rizzi, Benny Chia, Bruce Wasserman, Claudia Pozzana, Deepa Vanjani, Derek Lei, Dong Sun, Edward Tiesse, Elena Maria Blanco, Elizabeth Grobler, Elizabeth Libby Wong, Eva Brown, Florence Ng, Giorgio Bolla, Hasan Erkek, Hayley Ann Solomon, Henrik Hoeg, Indran Amirthanayagam, Jack Mayer, Janet Joyner, Joanna Radwańska-Williams, Jose Chambers, José Manuel Sevilla, Joyce Walker, Jun Pan, Kait Moller, Kate Hawkins, Keith Nunes, kerry rawlinson, Laura Potts, Laura Solomon, Lawrence Malu, Lee Ching Yin, Leung Ching Ning, Liam Blackford, Lucy Duggan, Luisa Ternau, Luke English, Lynda McKinney Lambert, Margus Lattik (Mathura), Marta Markoska, Maya Mitova, M. Ann Reed, Nick Compton, Paata Natsvlishvili, Paula Caronni, Peter Freckleton, Ho Cheung LEE (Peter), Psyche Chong, Roger Uren, Rony Nair, Sally Younger, Sandra Gibbons, Susan Lavender, Teresa N F Chu, Thomas Young, Viki Holmes, Vinita Agrawal, William Leo Coakley.

Editors
Gillian Bickley · Verner Bickley

Proverse Hong Kong

Mingled Voices 2
International Proverse Poetry Prize Anthology 2017
edited by Gillian Bickley.
1st published in Hong Kong by Proverse Hong Kong, April 2018.
Copyright © Proverse Hong Kong 2018.
Each author retains the copyright in the poem(s)
that appear with their own name(s).
ISBN: 978-988-8228-98-0

Distribution (Hong Kong and worldwide):
The Chinese University Press of Hong Kong,
The Chinese University of Hong Kong,
Shatin, New Territories, Hong Kong SAR.
E-mail: cup-bus@cuhk.edu.hk; Web: www.chineseupress.com

Distribution (United Kingdom):
Christine Penney, Stratford-upon-Avon, Warwickshire CV37 6DN, England.
Email: chrisp@proversepublishing.com

Also available from https://www.createspace.com/7553590

Distribution and other enquiries to:
Proverse Hong Kong, P.O. Box 259, Tung Chung Post Office,
Tung Chung, Lantau Island, NT, Hong Kong SAR, China.
E-mail: proverse@netvigator.com; Web: www.proversepublishing.com

The right of each writer to be identified as the author of the work(s) that
appear with their name(s) has been asserted by them
in accordance with the Copyright, Designs and Patents Act 1988.

Page design by Proverse Hong Kong.
Cover design by Pin-Key Design Co.

All rights reserved.
No part of this publication may be reproduced, stored in a retrieval system, or transmitted, in any form or by any means, electronic, mechanical, photocopying, recording or otherwise, without the prior written permission of the publisher. The book is sold subject to the condition that it shall not, by way of trade or otherwise, be lent, re-sold, hired out or otherwise circulated without the publisher's prior written consent in any form of binding or cover other than that in which it is published and without a similar condition including this condition being imposed on the subsequent owner or purchaser. Please contact Proverse Hong Kong in writing, to request any and all permissions (including but not restricted to republishing, inclusion in anthologies, translation, reading, performance and use as set pieces in examinations and festivals).

British Library Cataloguing in Publication Data.
A catalogue record for this book is available
from the British Library.

MESSAGE FROM VAUGHAN RAPATAHANA
First-prize winner,
inaugural
International Proverse Poetry Prize (2016)

It gives me considerable pleasure to pen a brief note regarding the new volume of *Mingled Voices*: the compilation of a diverse array of often polyglot voices, speaking to us across the pages via their panoply of tropes and topoi.

Well done to all pacesetter poets as represented within and especial congratulations to all the place-getters. Thank you also—of course—to Proverse, whose vision in creating and proselytising the poetry prize, I praise. I am certain that their endeavours will continue to flourish and that the Proverse Poetry Prize will continue to grow exponentially in terms not only of an increasing number of submissions from across the globe, but also of the growing recognition as a significant international literary award.

Indeed, I am certain that poets everywhere will come to covet representation within the pages, if they do not already!

Kia ora katoa [Thank you all].
Vaughan Rapatahana
Santo Tomas, Pampanga
Philippines
December, 2017.

ACKNOWLEDGEMENTS

All those at Proverse Hong Kong, administrators of the Proverse Poetry Prize (single poems), thank all those who entered for the 2017 competition, and warmly appreciate the helpful and willing participation in the editorial process of those whose poems were selected for this anthology.

We are most grateful, also, for the professionalism and dedication of the judges.

NOTE FROM THE EDITORS
and Proverse Poetry Prize Administrators

For this, the second annual international Proverse Poetry Prize, poems were invited, either on the entrant's own choice of subject or theme, or on a subject selected by the Proverse Poetry Prize Administrators, "Happiness" (interpreted as each entrant might wish). Any form, style or genre could be used.

Poems were judged by the panel of judges as submitted and the following awards were made:

First Prize
Jack Mayer, 'I Am A God To The Birds'
Second Prize
Margus Lattik (Mathura),
'Through the Eye of a Robinson's Needle'
Third Prizes
Vinita Agrawal, 'Home is Elsewhere';
Maria Elena Blanco, 'Interknitted';
Keith Nunes, 'A Juncture in Japan';
Edward Tiesse, 'Viet Nam Journey: Ha Noi Alley'.

Several other entered poems were awarded a place in this International Proverse Poetry Prize Anthology 2017, "Mingled Voices 2", and their names appear in the Table of Contents as well as the title page.

Congratulations to all!

Several of the poems in the Anthology were edited by the writers before publication, but no further judging of the entries was made at this stage.

All writers were invited to contribute a commentary or notes on their poems for this anthology and have responded in different ways.

Brief biographies of each of those whose work is represented in *Mingled Voices 2* are included in the anthology.

The places of birth of the writers whose work is included in this anthology range from Scandinavia to the Far East, to the southern hemisphere; and include Australia, Bulgaria, Canada, Cuba, Denmark, Estonia, Georgia, Hong Kong, Hungary, India, Italy, Macedonia, Macau, New Zealand, the People's Republic of China, Poland, South Africa, Spain, Turkey, the UK and the USA. Some have strong links with other countries, including East Germany and Zambia.

To the extent that those whose work is published here tell us about their professional lives, we know that some are University or College professors, including of Chinese Language and Literature, Drama, English, English Literature, Media Communications, Theory of Knowledge, Translation,. Some are lawyers, one is a barrister, another a diplomat. There is a paediatrician, a dentist, a publisher, an organisational consultant and manager, the director and founder of a contemporary arts space, an event management assistant. Some are students.

Entrants were asked to submit their work in English. To qualify, entries needed to be previously unpublished in English, but could have been previously published in another language.

For the 2016 anthology, *Mingled Voices*, poets were asked what language they wrote their poem in and gave very interesting answers which are recorded in that anthology. Some of the same poets have work in *Mingled Voices 2* (Maria Elena Blanco, Marta Markoska, Margus Lattik (Mathura), Angelo Rizzi, Dong Sun, Luisa Ternau). While the question was not asked on this occasion, in their brief biographies, included in this book, several have described the variety of languages that they know and/or write in. Indran Amirthanayagam writes in French, Spanish, Haitian Creole and Portuguese in addition to English. Maria Elena Blanco writes predominantly in her native Spanish. She translates her own poetry into English and has also developed her own English poetic voice in a style quite distinguishable from her Spanish one. Psyche Chong writes in both English and Chinese. Paata Natsvlishvili is the author of numerous books of poetry and essays in different languages. Angelo Rizzi's mother-tongue is Italian, but he is a polyglot poet writing in Italian, Spanish, and Arabic.

Several of the poets are or have been translators, interpreters, editors, teachers and/or students of the language and literature of other countries or cultural groups. Others teach translation, cross-cultural studies or communication. Several are well-travelled. Some are graphic artists and some are musicians. Some mention that poetry is only one of the literary genres that they write in.

As a group, these writers predominantly show an approach to life, thought, feeling, and artistic expression which extends beyond their specific place in the world, enabling them to exercise the "negative capability" that Keats spoke of, in different ways and prompted by different stimuli.

Some of the writers whose work appears in "Mingled Voices 2" are new or young writers. Others are already well-published as poets, whether in magazines and journals or in book form. Among them are prize-winning writers and writers who have participated in poetry festivals and other prestigious events.

Most writers chose to enter a poem on a subject or theme of their own choice although some did focus on the subject selected by the Proverse Poetry Prize Administrators, "Happiness". Each poem was judged on its own merits and those selected for this anthology are arranged simply in alphabetical order of poets' surnames and also by title. The poets' commentaries and notes on their poems, requested during the editing process, are presented as endnotes. The brief biographies of the poets (which were not known to the judges at the time of judging) appear in alphabetical order of poets' surnames.

Poems were invited in any genre or style. Most, but not all, are in free verse.

THE INTERNATIONAL PROVERSE POETRY PRIZE 2018

We very much hope that all who entered for the 2016 and 2017 International Proverse Poetry Prize and all whose poems are included here will continue to enter their work in future years. And of course we hope that others will join the competition in 2018.

Receipt of entries for the 2018 competition begins on 7 May 2018 with 30 June 2018 as the deadline.

As in previous years, poets may enter poems either on a subject or theme of their own choice or on the theme suggested by the Administrators for 2018, "Refuge", interpreted as each poet may wish. Full and updated details will always be available on the Proverse website, proversepublishing.com.

In the meantime, we hope those whose poems are included in the 2017 International Proverse Poetry Prize Anthology will enjoy seeing their and others' work and that all their readers will share the pleasure of the judges and the editors in these "Mingled Voices".

Gillian Bickley and Verner Bickley
Hong Kong

PREFACE

If, as the saying goes, variety is the spice of life, *Mingled Voices 2* offers a veritable feast. Not only are the authors drawn from many countries, as is immediately apparent from a glance at the table of contents, but their choice of theme is also pleasingly varied: while some explored the suggested idea of Happiness, many chose a different starting point.

One of the requirements for entry in this Proverse competition was brevity. It is noteworthy that, within the confines of a few lines, many of the authors were able to look past a simple scene or incident to some insight that sheds light on our relationship with the world we inhabit. Jack Mayer's 'I am a God to the Birds' does exactly that. He takes the everyday scene of the householder feeding the birds in his garden in winter, delighted by their beauty, and through their imagined perception of him as a Godlike creature, sees his own relationship with a God who feeds him spiritually, bringing beauty into his own life and sending him back "to holy books to peck at their words / for seeds of truth, for sustenance for exaltation". The seeming low key simplicity and quietness of tone are created and enhanced by the unobtrusive alliteration and the rhythm of his verse.

The work of the poets in this anthology is thought-provoking and interesting in the diversity of theme and approach. Margus Lattik's 'Through the Eye of a Robinson's Needle' imagines the experience of coming upon a new world in a remote island, never before glimpsed by the eye of man but existing from the beginnings: simply there, irrespective of man and his ambitions and activities. A Crusoe might have found himself washed up on its shores.

Elena Maria Blanco's poem 'Interknitted' impresses by the originality of its concept and by the subtle and accomplished way in which she clothes that concept. She employs the metaphor of knitting, where the creator of the garment is in total control of the strands of experience through time, creating whatever pattern suits her, undoing and changing as she rearranges the pattern. The short closing line "My doing" reinforces that suggestion of complete control.

Vinita Agrawal, in 'Home is Elsewhere', through a wealth of metaphor and telling imagery vividly presents the plight, experienced in so many countries, of the refugee desperately clinging to the smallest scraps of comfort in a new and dangerous world: the human spirit determined to survive. Edward Tiesse captures, in the brief confines of his poem 'Viet Nam Journey', the impact of a different, oriental way of life that still has recognisable basic similarities with a western pattern. In 'A Juncture in Japan' Keith Nunes handles, in a delicate and accomplished manner, a love affair that has come to an end: a sad parting no doubt, but eased by the happy and unquestioning acceptance of that parting by his hosts in a land and way of life far removed from his own.

Look further than the prize winners and find arresting cameos. Indran Amirthanayagam, in 'Yeats: Innocence, Experience', underlines the juxtaposition of the idyllic "paradise in green" and the "cluster attack" around the corner. Susan Lavender's 'The Dying Bride', in giving a human face to the ancient portrayal of Venice as bride of the sea, adds another layer of meaning: both human bride and architectural bride are crumbling into the waters. In 'Fire under Water' M. Ann Reed sees a universe in a maple leaf cupping rain drops; in 'Following the Life Force' she ponders the painter's impossible task of capturing "The peony's infinitely unfurling / coastline of repeating waves". Through his translator Helene Margaliti, Paata Natsvlishvili brings a lighter note and a touch of humour in 'Memory' with its witty re-iterations of "forget" and "forgetting". Hayley Ann Solomon in 'Happiness and I' revels in the elusive and carefree nature of happiness which should be shared and freely given to be fully enjoyed.

The reader often wonders what might have been the trigger for composition and very often there is no answer to that question. In *Mingled Voices 2* the writer's own notes can shed light on the creative process, sending the reader back to look again at the created work. It is a rewarding and pleasurable exercise.

Margaret Clarke,
Oxfordshire, UK

CONTENTS

Message from Vaughan Rapatahana, First Prize Winner in the inaugural Proverse Poetry Prize competition (2016)		5
Acknowledgements		6
Note from the Editors / Proverse Prize Administrators	Gillian Bickley, Verner Bickley	7
Preface	Margaret Clarke	11

POEMS

Vinita Agrawal	Home Is Elsewhere	19
Indran Amirthanayagam	Yeats: Innocence, Experience	20
Liam Blackford	Untitled	21
Elena Maria Blanco	Interknitted	23
Giorgio Bolla	Poetry Description	25
Eva Brown	Haploid Song	26
Paula Caronni	The Queer Eye	27
Jose Chambers	Bird Song in Hong Kong?	29
Benny Chia	Poem 1	30
Benny Chia	Poem 2	31
Benny Chia	Poem 3	32
Benny Chia	Poem 4	33
Psyche Chong	New Sun	34
Psyche Chong	Wake Up	36
Teresa N F Chu	Adele	38
Teresa N F Chu	Our Sweet Adele	39
William Leo Coakley	Waiting For Dusk	41
Nick Compton	Tai O	42

Lucy Duggan	Ovenproof	43
Luke English	On Leaving	44
Hasan Erkek	Limits Limit	45
Hasan Erkek	The Broken Wing of the Blues	46
Peter Freckleton	Zanzibar Love	48
Sandra Gibbons	For Joe	50
Sandra Gibbons	The Candle	51
Elizabeth Grobler	Road to Happiness	52
Elizabeth Grobler	Spirit of the Horse	53
Kate Hawkins	Distant Homes	55
Kate Hawkins	The Past Is Disappearing	56
Henrik Hoeg	The Tyrant's Garden	57
Viki Holmes	When we were kings of our castle	58
Janet Joyner	Upgivenhetssyndrome	60
Lynda McKinney Lambert.	Red December	61
Margus Lattik (Mathura)	Through the Eye of a Robinson's Needle	63
Susan Lavender	The Dying Bride	65
Lee Ching Yin	Anthem of Splendid Adventures	67
Ho Cheung LEE (Peter)	The Morning Call	69
Derek Lei	The Biggest Gamble	71
Leung Ching Ning	Sonnet of the Weird Sisters (*Macbeth*)	72
Lawrence Malu	Love	73
Marta Markoska	Spiced But Chilled	74
Jack Mayer	I Am A God To The Birds	75
Maya Mitova	Capriccio For Seven Heavens	76
Kait Moller	Flooding Home	77
Rony Nair	Juwairiya-5	78
Paata Natsvlishvili	Memory	79

Paata Natsvlishvili	Snow	81
Florence Ng	Aftermath	83
Keith Nunes	A Juncture in Japan	84
Jun Pan	Farewell, D!	85
Laura Potts	The Night That Robin Died	86
Claudia Pozzana	21st February 2002	88
Claudia Pozzana	I Never Call Myself	89
Claudia Pozzana	PEACE 安	90
Claudia Pozzana	Return, Sun	91
Claudia Pozzana	Tear	92
Claudia Pozzana	Theme: Missed Encounter	93
Claudia Pozzana	They Have Left	94
Claudia Pozzana	Two Rustled Up And Found Again Poems	95
Joanna Radwańska-Williams	Aerial View of Kunlun Mountains	96
kerry rawlinson	Aubade in May	97
M. Ann Reed	Echinacea Making Moonlight	99
M. Ann Reed	Fire under Water	101
M. Ann Reed	Following the Life Force	102
Angelo Rizzi	Today	104
José Manuel Sevilla	Voices in my head	105
José Manuel Sevilla	Silence is not sad	107
José Manuel Sevilla	Soul Cleaning	109
José Manuel Sevilla	Keys	111
Allegra Silberstein	Encounter	113
Hayley Ann Solomon	Happiness and I	114
Hayley Ann Solomon	Have I Found You, Utopia?	116
Hayley Ann Solomon	How do I love you? An Acrostic of Happiness	118

Laura Solomon	Four Walls	119
Dong Sun	Trestle	120
Abbie Taylor	Stay Away From MY Tree House	122
Luisa Ternau	Happiness on the Beach	123
Luisa Ternau	In Fear of Dusk	124
Luisa Ternau	Metropolitan Happiness	125
Luisa Ternau	Party Night	127
Edward Tiesse	Viet Nam Journey: Ha Noi Alley	128
Edward Tiesse	Viet Nam Journey: The Jade Pagoda	130
Roger Uren	Satan's Taxing Times	131
Deepa Vanjani	Happiness Entries in My Diary	132
Joyce Walker	Being Lost Along The Way	134
Bruce Wasserman	Elegy For My Father	135
Elizabeth Libby Wong	Gratitude	136
Thomas Young	An Angel's Kiss	137
Sally Younger	Interlude	138

Poets' Brief Biographies	139
Editors' Biographies	163
Proverse Hong Kong	169
Poets' Notes and Commentaries	171
Advance responses	203

Home Is Elsewhere[1]

Home, overnight, you are a step into the blind. A crammed safety-raft on choppy seas. A neighbourhood in Noah's canoe. A toddler wrapped in fleece blankets. Infant food in plastic pouches tucked into blouses. You are the fleeing, the landing, the reaching. A reluctant ribbon of earth. Land under swollen-raisin feet.

You are survivor bread wrapped in parachute nylon. Mildew and mould. In our skyward gaze, you are the cedars, the gumtrees, the open-beaked sunbird in a mangled nest. Padlocked songs of nightingales. Voiceless crayons rolling on tiles. And in the twilight hour, you are the serrated symmetry of sky against broken parapets.

You are submerged crypts of stars that predicted good fates. The satire. Tightly sewn skin of silence over cult. Visceral visions of hot toast and butter, cheese and brandy. Black coffee sipped on low wooden stools. The camaraderie of bi-lingual conversations across low boundary walls.

At the three a.m. hour, you are a vase, a door handle, fan blades, a secret hairpiece hooked behind an attic door, sheep in the pen, arms to long for, the lost compass, the hysteria that bursts forth from the aporia of taking the step into the blind.

In this camp of gashed fingers, brave faces, beggar hands, tear motifs, cold water through cheap taps, windy tents framing windows to a zilch destiny, godlike violations of hope velcroed to hunted-deer eyes, fresh fresh gravestones… you are a boldness that we dare to dream of.

Vinita Agrawal

Yeats: Innocence, Experience[2]

Peace comes dropping slow, Yeats wrote
in 'Innisfree'. I think of that bauble turning
in the show case window on Oxford Street,

poet away from home, passing by the music
box and stopping to remember an old scene,
a paradise in green, and leaving for generation

after generation his beauty unadulterated
by the unexpected trouble around the corner
of the shop, a pickpocket, a knife, or worse,

bomb ticking a popular tune, on everybody's
lips the number one hit, on the high street, a cluster
attack, in spite of early Yeats, Easter, 1916.

Indran Amirthanayagam
May 6, 2017

Untitled

Tradewinds from Hang Seng sea
Through market atria,
A grid of stone columns
Beveled with steel and chrome
Signs may glow above you
But they are mere symbols

Water dripping from rocks
A hand touching marble
Stone cold and resonant
Mouth open but no words
All vibrations reach pause
No message sent or seen.

Our range of difference
Distends beyond theory.
The things you find simple
Are what confound others
Yet the things that they say
Are all but noise to you.

Are we techno-enhanced
Techno-inhibited
Or techno-agnostic?
Are the systems we used
To construct our culture
Still now fit for purpose?

In a state of frenzy
No freedom too total
Bold and vociferous
Staring at a green light
Forging ahead with rage
Shameless and unafraid.

Liam Blackford

Interknitted[3]

I
Knit one, purl one: like saying
now a stick now a carrot, today
not yesterday, not ever, quasi tomorrow,
syllables ping-ponging over
the yarn, still life (oranges,
come autumn): like saying
check mate. Round off
cross stitch.

II
Rewind station:
major shift of scenery,
trade needle for crocodile
or gazelle skewer, wool for Egyptian
cotton, finely spun, flight. (Tedium).
Switch diet, switch mould and model,
mannequin.

III
The parts get tangled
(the plot thickens), reknit
edges, getaways, vindaloos—
the same wool, yes. Practice seed stitch,
braiding: kama sutra, pour
vodka in mango lassi.
Cast off front left,
slip right.

IV
During the halftime a dénoument creeps in—
cold-shower café-express intertwined
with hot-concocted delicacies:
curcuma, yoghourt, legumes,
finest Dutch skeins,
ice-cold beer. Lust.
Knots and cuffs still to be
done and undone.

My doing.

Elena Maria Blanco

Poetry Description[4]

The route of a
poem
joins together
the senses
because it flies
beyond any fondness
and, to its way of thinking,
it goes in the head
so it can break, sometimes.
Then it goes back,
like in a circle,
but changed,
unlike.
Without the tinsels
of the mind, maybe,
anyone could
follow it,
within its
flight.

Giorgio Bolla

Haploid Song

I fit where I was born

I am a fish in the water
a snail on a leaf
a mole in a burrow
a shag on a rock
flea on a dog
hawk in the sky

I was born
on this planet
into this age
this era
I inhale its inevitable air
soak up its sounds and smells

I am a fish in ebbing water
a hawk in a tarnished sky
I don't know why
don't know
why

Eva Brown

The Queer Eye[5]

You were still a seed,
Floating in my womb
In search of fertile soil,
And I was unaware that
Many years later, I would have to come back to you
When my eye popped out of its socket.

In the blink of *that* eye
You had changed, transformed, grown up;
A foreigner in her own land,
Who spoke an incomprehensible language
Or none at all.

Was I trying too hard to look beyond,
Penetrate the unknown realm of a fledgling mind,
See through the door of your inaccessible space
Desiring you to grow
Without so much pain,
To flourish, bloom
Without severing your roots?

The queer eye did not see, could not see,
Despite the efforts, the squinting and the straining.
The eyelid—exhausted—started swelling.
And I often woke up at night with my cheek wet
Of tears unknown.
Other times, I had double vision: and it was the two of you,
The one I knew well, and the one I did not.

Finally, the bulging eye strayed,
Pulled up the lid and exposed the bulb,
Like an actor naked on stage,
Who never went back to his old home.

Still now, as it painfully focuses on things past,
It yearns to catch sight of
A young girl, in her mother's arms,
Whose dark and piercing gaze relaxes
To the melodious sound of a familiar voice.

Paula Caronni

Bird Song in Hong Kong?

Sunday in Hong Kong:
The tight spaces between
High rise towers
Are filling up….

Chattering flocks of women
Cluster, perch,
Cut each other's hair,
Share photographs:
Talking, talking...

"Who are they?"
"Why so many?"
"Look—everywhere!"

Maids, cooks, shop girls,
Far from home;
Migrant birds,

Out….

For the day.

Jose Chambers

Poem 1[6]

I will die in Paris
But not when it rains.
Not when the bus is full of
Old people squabbling for the only seat.
French spoken too quickly and too loud.
Not when the museums are full of tourists like myself
Blocking everyone's view for a photo shoot.
Not when the parks are left with skeletons for trees.
After I am dead
Please don't bury me with rows upon rows of
strangers.
Just scatter my ashes in
The Jardin du Luxembourg.
Preferably on a warm and sunny day
When lovely flowers bloom.
But please don't do it in the winter night,
When the ground is much too hard
To receive what remains of me.

Benny Chia

Poem 2

We too stood waiting in the long line
For the next bus that might not come.
It came.
We got home.
To each other's home.
In the long howling storm
We all slept alone
Longing for dawn
And the storm to blow over.

Benny Chia

Poem 3

Between the concrete slabs
In the canyon of cagey tall buildings
Matted with cold lights and washings
You catch a glimpse of the moon
Each night getting fuller
Breasts swelling
Rounding teats rising to
Exploring fingertips
Pores oozing beads of sweat
On the icey silver surface
Once bubbling in molten rocks.
The pain gripping
Gut wrenching that foretell
Plentiful life has in store
For each and every eager soul
To burst into this world.

Benny Chia

Poem 4

The sun scorches the chequered concrete floor
Straight long walk offering no shelter.
Don't let the heat rising from below bake your limbs.
Or that from above crack your skull.
Let it open the pores of the skin
On the bones of your ancient body.
Soak it up,
Soak it all up.
To warm you and the sleepy one
Lying next to you
In wintry nights.

Benny Chia

New Sun[7]

You mourned
for your broken heart caused
by uncountable attacks blown
stripping all the leaves
disenchanting your desired dream

You go forth
nakedly wailed in the wind
silently bowed your knees
so to end
the distraught terminal fist

Can you tell
how your wound will be healed
My love, give me a hint
as I'm lost in
what can I give

Replant you a twinned trees
Rebuild you a ranch cabin
Tightly hold your hands
Let not you grieve in the bleakness
I do everything for you, in my senses

And you, please
Believe your dream
Keep intact the spirit
Stretch out your arms
Embrace the bliss

The dark has gone
New sun ensues
This is the rule
with the other eternity
is my consistency for you

Psyche Chong

Wake Up

Murky room penetrated with dead air
Till a toot from downstairs
Piercing silence
The doctor said funeral be prepared
Not much time left

Left, I thread through the pack
Sunbeams sparkle peoples' heads
Hips in tights are swinging
But I hear nothing
For now I go deaf

Deaf and I can't stand
Something wants me to collapse
Air, I snatch
Nothing in my hand
I fall at the end

End, what's wrong with that
Vaguely hear God reflect
"Forget your mortgaged shell
And ritzy bags
Come back"

Back, why want me back
Kindergarten bell has rung yet
On the ground I weep
Reach out to Facebook the thousand friends
Oh WeChat, which we I can chat and connect

"Connect a few, is that"
A voice said when I up my head
Unwittingly the sky has turned pale
Someone honks, waken me up to stand again
For the few I have

Psyche Chong

Adele[8]

To Adele, my personal canine therapist when I turn into an animal—the raging bull

How stubborn of you, my silly girl,
To choose to stay with this master turned monster,
A raging bull boiling and bursting with anger,
Sickly spilling rabid foams of terror.

Cursing life, cursing fate, cursing all matters that do not matter,
This willful master wields some wrecking power.
Yet without a cower, you calmly station yourself at the epicenter,
Doggedly determined to sit through all the unnecessary human drama.

Your amber eyes quietly plead with an offer of yourself
To guard against the threat of haemorrhage that evil spells.
With every stroke on your body is a riot quelled,
And the master's woeful wrath is soon dispelled.

Thank you, my girl, for bravely choosing to stay in my arms
When the whole wide world would just scatter in red alarm.
Adele, my loving guardian angel with such therapeutic charm,
You are my pride, my joy, and my eternal psalm.

Teresa N F Chu

Our Sweet Adele (2003-2017)[9]

April/May 2017
Our sweet Adele, she's unwell.
Her mouth swells from a massive mass that smells.
Blood drips from the deadly cells.
The floor now speaks of hell.
Her soft bed too has horror tales to tell.
Our sweet Adele, she needs some help.

Our sweet Adele.
Let us clean and dry your blood-matted coat.
Let us catch those nasty drips from your pretty nose.
Let us stay close so we can closely watch our lovely rose.
Let us take you to Dr Justin, for the best advice and medicine.
Let us buy you more healthy snacks, and all the necessary supplements.
Let us in tiny portions deliver your daily meals on a spoon
As life goes on, surely, with the sun, the stars and the moon.
Let us care for you now, for as long as God would allow.
Let us enjoy your gentleness and your beauty
As you honour and privilege us with your company.
What a blessing, to be together, in our small loving family.

18 May 2017
Alas, our sweet Adele, finally gone.
Sadly we grieve, and for a long time we shall mourn.
Thanks, dear, for your love and the bliss of your sweet final loving kiss.
Thanks for the many wonderful memories that we shall all dearly miss.
You have been the family's greatest gift,
And personally my strongest lift.
The rainbow bridge you will cross it well.
There, kind angels await with loving arms
And you will forever be safe from harm.
We love you, forever and longer.
Our bond shall be as always, just much stronger.
Adieu, Adele; Au revoir, ma belle.

Teresa N F Chu

Waiting For Dusk

Five old men, too wise to go home,
Sit at a table, the wine almost gone.
Whatever you ask us,
Don't believe what we say:
We lost a world of wonder
Through our own fault—of age.
The last drops and sips are done,
But we won't want you to guide us.
Off we go to the river together
To watch the sun as it sets
A golden road on the water to walk on
We don't need yet.

William Leo Coakley

Tai O

Together, we traversed
    the gangplanks
        and artificial pathways
of the ancient sea village,
    the warped wood
        lamenting our foreign presence.
    Below, crabs carved empires
in the drying flake-mud while
    a salt riddled wind
        brought heat and an incense
            of fish, luring our lean stomachs.

In the company of locals
    my brother and I
        delved into our rubbery meal
of fish balls,
        our teeth sinking into spicy white flesh
            as we waited for the bus
                to Tian Tan.

Nick Compton

Ovenproof[10]

This is a series of words
about the way to make bread.
This is a simple kit:
she serves up ox tongue and foxgloves,
a family tea, a kitchen corner.

Dream that you know how to bake it,
knead the dough,
dream that you homemake it every week, every night.

She wrote instructions.
She wrote numbers round the dials on the oven.
She wrote loving stubborn covenants in rhyme
and sticky iambics, she poked them in like raisins,
and she made loaves as hard as diamonds,
she made this bed among the shriveled scraps of
dough,
she made bread and love in this machine.
Look at it prove, there is not room for two
in this tin. Ask the writer to slide it in,
graze the top with a cross.

Clouds thud down, and the dandelions are moulting.
Bite your lion's teeth together and chew bread,
chew sorrel and remember,
chew nettles and forget,
forget the recipe.
Leave it unsaid, unbroken, unproved.
It rises,
it cracks.
There is the distance:
there is the sky which stays raw in the heat.

Lucy Duggan

On Leaving

In the purple morning, He walks away.
Against His thigh, the grass;
Above His eye, the sky.
Below His feet, the blood;
With Her inside his mind.
In the air were birds with calls that synchronize.
In His heart was not but cold and iron, dry.
The singing head between His ears, did ring;
Red footsteps in the dew, behind.
A rapture close at hand draws nigh,
Setting night upon a dying sky.
Thunder in His legs makes still, his nervous feet to run;
And again, the birds sing loud and cry to the rising sun.
Her voice is in his head and blood around his toes,
That are walking through the grass where the crickets seldom go.
In the sky is red where purple once did hang;
Clouds gone down to show the bloody thing,
That sits where once the sun did shine.
On His thigh, the light.
Above His eye, the blood.
Below His feet, the sky.
With Her inside his mind.

Luke English

Limits Limit

You may surmount the mightiest peak
only to face your soul where tiny streets meet,
towering before you like a mountain

You turn into a river that rushes to the sea
yet the drop you become is no remedy
for your wounds; you dry up in your own desert

You burn ships, blow up bridges
only to buttonhole yourself with your own hand,
unable to bring down the walls of your mind

Your fire reduced to ashes, your song heard no more,
your path complete
You end up leaning on yourself
Reaching into yourself

Searching for hope in your depths

Hasan Erkek

The Broken Wing of The Blues

A winter morning breaks, kissing your forehead with
its cold lips
awakening you from serene dreams
while the wind rests its wings on your window
from the misty horizon looms the sun hazy-eyed,
not that you can have a stretch and raise a smile

Snow must have frozen on the roofs and puddles
turned to ice on the roads
even your latest photographs you consign to the past
a cord of sorrow wrapped around your waist, you gaze
at your silhouette on a tea glass
while a cello concerto strolls around the walls of your
room
the sun will always rise, that's for sure,
not that you can brush away your worries into the light

Standing across from your mind is a long-expected
lover
even if she had come, she wouldn't have been robed in
poetry
out of nothing, her crystal voice would have lost its
clarity
the thin ankles of her words would have sprained
for everything there is but one answer, inscribed in the
membrane of the tongue,
not that she will reveal it or you discover it

Mornings bereft of love are eyelids deprived of sleep
you resent the darkness that clings to those mornings
and recall more cheerful days,
friendships in the distant backyards of your memory,

songs echoing in wells,
every last one of them piling up on you as each year
follows the previous
you will come to terms with it all, that's for sure,
not that life grants you a gentle breeze, a chance to rest

Hasan Erkek

Zanzibar Love[11]

Life is sweet in Zanzibar,
A lovely land where good things are.
People there eat abalone,
Lotus leaves and honeyed eels
Rosy-red with cinnabar,
And after those, zabaglione.

No-one there but sups such meals
Reclining by a samovar.

So fresh and pure the milk
They pour from silvern ewers,
Its white is hued with pale azure.

Nothing there wants in Zanzibar,
Fleet xebecs bear brimming jars
Of wine to flow in shady bars.

Zithers they play and dulcimers,
With ocarina celestinas
To the beat of xylophones.

The note so suave
Senses swoon
When drowsing breezes
Sift their freight
Of harmonied perfume.

No kings are known but only queens,
Rulers all, Zanzibareens.
Surrounded each by male harems,
They finger unforbidden fruit,
One caress and one deny.
For men must please in Zanzibar.

Life is sweet in Zanzibar—
Save for the sweep of the scimitar.

Peter Freckleton

For Joe[12]

Love has no definition and it never follows any rules.

It washes with kindness, ever thoughtful
feel the tenderness, with grace does it listen,
going deep into we who are there,
the head tilts
perception with incision

See not its fine features, see a soul
hear the words like music and laughter,
mesmerizing with meaning that captures,
absurdity in the real
the beauty of the unreal

It rides in slow motion, no sound
movement to harmony, with thoughts in a breeze,
taming those who are around,
in a trance
held in time with heart's beat

Love has no definition and it never follows any rules.

Sandra Gibbons

The Candle[13]

The candle went out again last night
No warning—just dark

From a haven of warmth
A mother's embrace
Her smile filled with sunshine, leading the way
Telling me truths, showing me how
Strong and alive, standing upright

To a cavern of coldness
Darkness enfolding
Her words laced with poison, curdle my soul
Falling to silence, leaving me all alone
Broken and shattered, crawling away

Till the wick starts to flicker
No warning—just light

In the haven of warmth
No longer secure
My breath draws slowly, trembling inside
Forever loving, arms reaching out
Watching and waiting, till life stops again.

Sandra Gibbons

Road to Happiness[14]

Responsibility, for joy, rests on your shoulders,
Others' opinions shouldn't be boulders.
Altruistic acts of compassion in everyday life,
Deeds of love and avoidance of strife.

Transforming your every thought
    from stumbling block to stepping stone,
Overcoming obsessions and fears with help,
    and strength of your own.

Happiness heartily found in every moment, causing
    contentment to grow
Attitude or mindset could serve as an ally or foe.
Patience, peace of mind and peace on Earth,
Passion accompanied by purpose
    resonate your true worth.
Integrity revealed through immaculate behaviour,
    not beliefs nor words,
Noble and kind acts done discreetly, unseen, unheard.
Excitement and gratitude for each new day,
    equal enthusiasm for work and play.
Spending time with sublime people
    who make you feel special and bright,
Sunny smiles that shatter dark sadness
    and bring forth splendid light.

Elizabeth Grobler

Spirit of the Horse[15]

Dedicated to my son Alrik Victor Grobler, who was born on 9 January 2015, the Year of the Horse in the Chinese Zodiac.

From The Source
your brilliant spirit
descended into
dark water.

There you took shape with your own unique life force.
A delicate seahorse with your tail anchored to me,
Sensitive and responsive,
patient, content and carefree.

From the dark water to your new ground,
you ascended into the stark light.
Walk, trot, canter and gallop with boisterous sound!
A noble steed embarking on its own journey,
a fresh start.
Untainted and enthusiastic,
impatient, strong, spirited heart.

You'll want to roam free
and conquer your next terrain.
Speed towards your brilliant future,
with clear vision and focus,
towards a greener endless plain.
A wise unicorn,
seeking the gateway to a higher sphere of unity,
insight and divine consciousness.
A virtuous seeker of merit and harmony.

In the end you'll depart
and reach your Elysian field.
You'll swiftly rise and soar into illumination,
carrying only the knowledge
and the great spiritual power that you wield.
A heavenly Pegasus,
that drew forth inspiration, creativity and ecstasy,
Friend of the Muses and immortal soul,
beautiful spirit,
fly free!

Elizabeth Grobler

Distant Homes[16]

Distant	Homes
pretty little boy	pretty little girl
built houses of dreams	watching stars
he lies in fields	singing pretty songs of sadness
crying for Singapore	not knowing Hong Kong anymore
the home he adored	now just a distant spot in an atlas

Kate Hawkins

The Past Is Disappearing[17]

The past is disappearing,
The future is appearing,
The distant cries,
The tears from my eyes,
Are somehow leaving,
But by my side the past is still alive,
And always it will be in my mind.

Kate Hawkins

The Tyrant's Garden

If the flowers fail to listen
Do not shed a tear for them,
They have made their own decision
To be taken root and stem.

Let the flowers hang from gallows,
Have them face the firing squad,
Bring them to the guillotines,
They can make their peace with God.

Bring the flowers to the chambers,
There to breathe the toxic fumes,
Spare no tulip, rose or orchid,
Lest they come into their blooms.

Let the flowers be injected,
With what poisons we concoct,
Let them sit on cushy chairs,
To receive electric shocks.

Let the lilies fare no better,
Let them break beneath the rod,
Tie them to the whipping post,
So all can witness and applaud.

Let them die upon the cross,
Have them hung and drawn and quartered,
When they see such consequences,
Have no doubt they'll do as ordered.

Henrik Hoeg

When we were kings of our castle[18]

When we were kings of our castle
the tents below spawned like small aliens

on the beach's spread. Everyone
quested for fire but we were top of the world,

and we delighted
in the algebra of twigs.

On the hot stones we boiled water,
roasted fish. The stars began.

Next day we quested,
looking for pools.

I was scared, for the first time
I'd never been so high.

I couldn't see the end of things.
It hurt me. If I'd not slipped

we might have made it.
I lost confidence.

You were a map-maker,
I, squabbling with mosquitos

as you ascended, the trees
closed around me, I lost the river.

We made it. Below, in the yawning tide
we stumbled into salt.

Stung into living again,
remembering how to submerge.

Viki Holmes

Upgivenhetssyndrome

Thirteen-year-old Georgi,
in his boxers and athletic
socks, lies mute and senseless
on his bed in Garpenberg,
one hundred and twenty miles
northwest of Stockholm.
Like Snow White, Georgi
has fallen away from this world.
The condition he now exhibits
is showing up in emergency rooms
filled with teenage, Syrian refugees
whose asylum status has expired.
Georgi, for his part, would rather
lie down and die. The Swedes
now even have
a word
for it.

Janet Joyner

Red December

New-fallen snow glimmers in pre-dawn darkness
slender red barberries dangle from thin bare branches
I shuffle my feet, dig in to feel solid ground
near the place where my Father's red roses
are surrounded by pillows of snow
slumbering safe in dark red December.

My heavy suede boots part the snow
It's too early for the red cardinals
"Where do they go at night?"
A sharp wind makes me huddle deeper into my bright
red bouclé jacket
while my two dogs search random trails
follow the long marks, meander downhill.

On a crisp day in mid-December
I desire red raspberry jam on warm toast
Linger by the tall pampas grass
weighted down to the ground with icy snow
I think of strawberry Sundays with whipped cream
I recall wearing Neiman Marcus Red lipstick and
dancing all night in
hot red stilettos and tight blue jeans.

We turn around—for the return home
the dogs circle in the frozen pachysandra patches
stiff, brown-green shrunken leaves.
In memories I see my neighbour walking to her car
she wears a cranberry red hat, worsted red wool coat,
flat, scarlet red shoes
carries a true-red leather handbag like the one I bought
last Sunday.

I watched her from the upstairs window.
In her 80s, she revealed how to live a gallant life.

No cars pass us on the country road this morning in red
December
Where it is perpetual winter.

Lynda McKinney Lambert

Through the Eye of a Robinson's Needle[19]

I came here solitary. I leave amused.
—Pedro Amarino, *500 Days without Civilization*

Noon and its heat—
you can't put in a can,
can't wrap the scent of flowers
in tinfoil or paper.
Waves crushing on the precipice
cannot be lifted
unto a dugout on blue water.

Seven thousand silhouettes
inside a single island,
the white ash of sand,
and songs oozing from the heights
of eucalypti just like honey,
voices richer than they themselves
would dare to believe;

a single resting place
and seven thousand ways of knowing
lands golden, green and purple, blue,
uninhabited,
but brimming with life—
crabs lurking in the shallows, time
crawling back into its motley shell—

a world that's been forgotten
and then re-dreamt of,
a Robinson the only man still there to know:
soul's horizons
never reach their conclusion,
explorers of spirit
never find their final rest.

Margus Lattik

The Dying Bride[20]

Once again she stands ready
To meet her groom.
Ever less steady,
She awaits her inevitable doom.

She recalls, many moons ago, the first time,
No father to defend her, she yielded to his salty slime,
A child bride, buoyed by enthusiasm: virgin, pristine,
Ravishing, not ravished, shiny and clean.
This year, as each year on Ascension Day, they renew their vows.
Stooping ever more arthritically, to her lord and master she bows,
As a wedding ring drops in water, to the crowd's applauding roar.
It's just one more briny notch on his ancient score
Against his now aging, but ever elegant, whore.
She's no longer a maid,
She's just simply decayed.
She's ravaged and raped, she's battered and bruised,
But as he devours her, seasoned with salt, he's quietly amused.

Giant cement hands prop up her osteoporotic plight,
But they can't withstand her gradual crumbling, sinking into the night.
He says: *"Surrender to me, don't you see, I won't let you stand taller than me."*
He persists. Faithful, as always, she can't resist.
She says: *"I choose not liberty, but thee"*.
She has no choice, she has no voice.

He doesn't want her on top of him.
He's dragging her down slowly into his lagoon.
He wants her beneath him,
To be submerged, very soon.

Venice, bride of the Sea, abused wife of the Sea,
Soon to be a drowned bride city *under* the Sea.

Susan Lavender

Anthem of Splendid Adventures[21]

What boredom I see in the eyes
Of people who have ceased to live!
Hollow dreams in empty lives,
So dull it reaches the infinite abyss.

What dread I smell in the living dead
And minds rotten by office desks!
Thrill and joy is what they seek,
Like crabs in rayless holes they peek.

Ought we not to enjoy sunshine?
Shan't we experience the rain?
Life is an infinite adventure,
Let's not cease exploring new terrain!

Follow that enigmatic kiwi bird,
Drift away with the Australian herd.
Sail to uncharted creeks and seas,
Find out where Atlantis might be!

Raft along the raging Nile,
Hands on paddle, let's be bold!
Cruise beside the historic Thames,
Visit abbeys, the kingdom's gems and gold.

Hungry and dry, the Sahara fiercely cries,
"My daunting sandstorm's beyond the sky!"
The multi-coloured Amazon beams at you,
"I've got piranhas, jaguars and stunning views!"

Mount Everest, frosty and cruel,
"Behold my fangs and my blizzard's duel."
Over the ridges lies the Dragon's Great Wall,
"My aged brick back will never fall."

Picturesque places kindling great wonder
Are telling us not to dwell on the ground
For life is dear! Let's make it count!
God's work is meant to grandly astound!

What passion I hear in inquiring souls
Singing upbeat anthems, ready to glow!
So let's get packed and instantly go!
Pluck up our courage! Attain all our goals!

Lee Ching Yin

The Morning Call[22]

failed again for the third time this term.
The room'd over-coloured as the final ring

came through. I dived to the door with my chest
barely clad. A double-sided jacket wrapped

all the loose buttons as I almost ejected my
car from the second level. Traffic lights brutally

turned my song into frantic horns. I hit 120 on
the highway to limit the time by which I arrived

late to a minute seventeen seconds. I did blame
the traffic, the ill-timed temperature, my death.

But they should have been there, receiving
the morning like they used to, piercing into

my reincarnation, those programmed directives.
And murmurs from their joints. Coughs.

Since when should I have realized the cart had
ceased running on the snow? The tracks filled

and the gallops grew distant. My room had
wordlessly crept into its last season.

This morning the laughter dragged me to
the windows. My boy easily mocked the

backyard of snow, stretching on the lawn chair,
shirtless. His wool hat and old jeans

emphasized the sunlight on his hairless skin.
The late tune from the alarm.

I coiled back into the landscape of bedding,
checked with the frame-filtered February ray.

The toilet flushes.
Those knocks.

Ho Cheung LEE (Peter)

The Biggest Gamble

I'm not so arrogant to say that
there's no god,
I just don't know
which of the many
versions out there
is true.

and to blindly believe in
and devote oneself
to just one of them
is the
biggest gamble there is.

Derek Lei

Sonnet of the Weird Sisters (*Macbeth*)[23]

Among the hills the fog doth blind our sight;
In valley shrills the wind and wolves surround,
But smother not the venomous green light,
Where sings my sisters' art inferno-bound.
Say "Double, double toil and trouble" thrice,
A storm in cauldron spurts a dusty breath.
Thus humbly read of its prepense device:
Foretell the fate of man whose name Macbeth!
Too thickened blood upon my sisters' kin,
With artful riddles cast his last presage.
But mortals blame us for deceitful sin,
Know not of what their hearts and souls engage.
    To think there is a deed without a name,
      O child, now come and meet eternal flame!

Leung Ching Ning

Love

Love.
Love is love.

Love is irresistible feelings of one
towards another one.
Love is for all.
Love all, serve all.
This is the way of the lord.
Love moves the world.
Without love
Life is in vain.
Without love all is lost,
for love helps us to move forward in real life.
So love all, serve all.
This is the way of the lord.

Lawrence Malu

Spiced But Chilled[24]

If someone can describe your body
wrapped in a sheet
while I am trying to write
my female contours on your manliness
other might contradict and say
that I am not a creative but a selfish artist
thinking only how to put a self-note
a footnote
a sign
as if I possess your body
as a work of art, as an icon
wanting love to be immortalized
and preserved from decaying

If someone can describe your nudity
Better than me, while we are wrapped
like a taco and our sauces taste
like bitter-sweet vanishing,
then you should be someone else's sculpture,
and I…
I should be but a leaf that
accidentally covered your manliness

Marta Markoska

I Am A God To The Birds[25]

I am a God to the birds
flocking to my feeder in the winter.
A forgiving God who,
when winter winds bite
and the summer's bounty is frozen,
miraculously provides fishes and loaves,
sunflower seeds and suet,
in exchange for their beauty,
their bickering, their blessing.
They cannot know how I praise them
through the glass, astounded
that they can fly and I cannot,
that for them fear is so ordinary,
so transcendent, that they proclaim
the glory.

When the winter of my soul chills,
when the fruits of summer are exhausted,
I turn to holy books to peck at their words
for seeds of truth, for sustenance, for exaltation.
I revel in the mystery, the prayer that a God
behind the window enjoys me enough
to feed my soul.

Jack Mayer

Capriccio For Seven Heavens[26]

When you hold me
I stretch my silences in bliss
and see how sharply pointed
the towers outside have grown.
Our day is then an island,
from its shores swan tales fly
fluttering in the long-haired roads
and white cloudy silences.
Then my pulse starts racing in you
on the seven strings of light,
drives you crazy with capriccio.
It collects the yolks and whites
of light in the two halves of the shell,
breathlessly weaving shirts
the unified to cloak.
It flies seven times over your island—in a circle,
driven by the whisper of an ocean of reeds.
It puts wedding dresses on the waves—
releases the princes out of their swans.
Then the towers turn into fairies
with conical hats and wings.
With transparent ring
they send flying pollen in our hands.
They attract the gentle planets
to embrace, and such embrace I wouldn't give
for a kingdom, the same embrace,
which makes two people jump
into the paraglider—towards the seven skies.

Maya Mitova

Flooding Home[27]

I come from Se-Port and train rides,
flowing from city to city,

though my map has always been skewed
you took a chance on a home one night

I saw you, I watched you write it in your lungs
with a cigarette, forgetting about Montauk

when your smoke danced toward the end
of a home not worth living in

and a bay filled with Natural Bohemian
ebbing from north to south
with careful fingertips and a single match
saying *this is your future,*
shoving a pen into my hand
as I laid in a field with someone who wasn't you
where those careful fingertips wrote me a tune,
and chose an addiction for its title:
a town not for staying in.

Kait Moller

Juwairiya-5[28]

this was not what we signed up for.
a life lived—middle of the hoard
banking on castoffs, craving on mime.

outrage in portions. doled out
recycle bins, of the mind.
loose ends without kite strings tethered
bleating blind leading the blind

rafts run over half strewn gossip
tidal waves uproot ferments from the mind
right armpits coalesce in parade
they all feel alive. with the past in rewind.

craggy shop fronts, feel good cliffs
mirrors of empty shrapnel tins,
burnt scavengers hold broken images
tuna can covers, old memory banks!

this was not what we signed up for.
shrapnel in piecemeal
your head, for a dime.

Rony Nair

Memory[29]

I can't ever forget you.

Even if I forget you,
I will still remember how I forgot you.
I can't ever forget you.

Even if I forget that I forgot you,
I will still remember how I forgot
Forgetting you.
I can't ever forget you.

Even if I forget that I forgot
Forgetting you,
I will still remember how I forgot
To forget forgetting you.
I can't ever forget you.

Even if I forget that I forgot
To forget forgetting you,
I will still remember how I forgot
To forget forgetting
To forget you.
I can't ever forget you.

Even if I forget that I forgot
To forget forgetting
To forget you,
I will still remember how I forgot
To forget forgetting
To forget forgetting you.
I can't ever forget you.

Even if I forget you…
I can't ever forget you.

Paata Natsvlishvili
Translated from Georgian by Helene Margaliti

Snow[30]

I'll come at three o'clock at night
And I'll lay an ambush in each house I pass by.
Snow is worth more
When it's already snowed at dawn.

I go up and up slowly
And too carefully
So that the earth won't get tired,
So that the sleep won't get scared
Out of your town.

So that the earth won't get tired,
So that the sleep won't get scared
Out of your town,
With my weakness and not my strength
I'll lift your town up now.

You will wake up early
And you will be trembling
While opening the windows
And you will suppose
That the snow in your yard
Is just snow.

You love the innocent colour of snow,
You look for the childish drawings in snow,
You see me and your exhausted glance
Is leaving footprints on my chest.

Don't ask me who I am or what,
Early morning you'll meet me in the town.
I'll be marvelously warm
In the frightening freeze around.

Paata Natsvlishvili
Translated from Georgian by Helene Margaliti

Aftermath

Someone complained about bird droppings.
Officers came with a grenade
to punish the tree.
The chicks rained
like fried nuggets.
Eggs became bean curd.
Problem solved.

Some winds stopped by,
whispered in each other"s ears,
and added this to their travel journal
among "vegetarian tiger", "talking penguin",
"masquerade of chimps".
Before they moved on they laid
a few rusty leaves
to rot with the scene.

Florence Ng

A Juncture in Japan[31]

the sake was hot
held the warmth
of his small hands
disfigured by land and time,
he put a hand on my shoulder
"ippai yarimasu"
so I swallowed the cup's contents

in the spring morning
pounding head on
blossom pillow

his daughter in a green kimono
dances on the path in
wooden geta sandals that clack and crack
like erratic clapping

"ohayō gozaimasu" she says
"yes, good morning to you"

the man of the house
waves from his plough
his wife
charting their accounts
on a laptop

the broad farmed valley
falls away to the sea

the hurt of yesterday
has vanished,
the cut was clean
she is not coming back

Keith Nunes

Farewell, D![32]

A restless night
Memories of over 4,000 days
You were absent in my dreams

Two lines from your email address
I typed my words
Only to erase them afterwards

The Christmas cruise I did not join
Sails to the summer we never meet
Maple leaves around my feet

You always reminded me how special I am
Across the other side of the ocean
From the land with a sexy name

Now it is my turn
To keep thoughts of you
When I look at stars in heaven

Jun Pan

The Night That Robin Died[33]

I remember it best as burnt lips and black
that night when the mouth of the house spat
you and your terminal news out to the stars
and back. Before the last evening hours
had passed, flame yielding life to the ember,
the crack of your ash called a duskdark September
too soon to its spring. It was the summer to never

remember. Robin, that radio screamed all the night
like your ambulance light living on and tight
was my wren-clenched flesh, was the glut
in my throat for you, lost-light bird never cut
from the cage. The age that was yours was the loudest
and long, but that old August day blew its dust
far on past those bones growing epigraph-grey:
a memento that death is just one storm away.

These days, one more last-light life blown out,
the heart in my body beats that much more loud.
Oh gallow-bound you with the ballroom grin,
for each crowd at your feet another rose out in
a mutual call, a language too dark for the masses
at all. That fall from the world, as springtime passes
its breath to the last, was the black blacker blackest

that my past has carried. After that passage, dusk
    folded
and wearied away, I stood at the gate summer-coated
to wait, watching your far-flaming ghostlight fade.

You never doubted the fire that flared, that made
you a light living on in that night. While bone-body
    dies
and we look to the stars bygone-bright in your eyes,
know only your laughter lit hearthstone and home.
Know yours is the name never lost from the stone.

Laura Potts

21st February 2002[34]

To Silvia

far, yet in the flesh
    we meet again to keep the
        accounts of wrinkles
  at times we can hardly
      understand each other
but a shiny and invisible thread
      like a spiderweb
keeps together thoughts and memories,
with sentences said or withheld,
and we preserve it hanging in
its corner inside our hearts

Claudia Pozzana

I Never Call Myself[35]

I never call myself
I listen, I talk to myself,
at times I criticize myself, yet
I never ever call my own self

Claudia Pozzana

PEACE 安[36]

AN, 安 say the Chinese
and it is an ancient peace
that is wished
draws a roof
under which a woman stays
an ancestral peace
not certainly ensured
today coveted
with fatigue unhoped for peace
that like a war
may be declared

Claudia Pozzana

Return, Sun[37]

I am a "cartina di tornasole",*
a litmus paper,
In touch with pain
I retrace my steps
Incapable of changing
With the evil of the world before me.

Torna sole or tourne soleil?
If anything, in touch with love
I shine full of sun like a sunflower
A wing to the summer song of cicadas
Golden like a tourist.

A "tornasole" paper
Changes mood and colour
Yet night does not know colours
Nothing seems to change
Only silence is interrupted.

Claudia Pozzana

*Translator's note: litmus paper in Italian is "cartina di tornasole". The word tornasole is composed of the verb tornare, to return in "torna", and "sole", the Italian word for sun.

Tear[38]

Tear in the scrubs
of the sick,
skinned heart shrieks

life regardless
in silence
vehemently laughs

Claudia Pozzana

Theme: Missed Encounter[39]

Development:
unthinkable
without chance's help
make a pact
without contractors

Claudia Pozzana

They Have Left[40]

For Ottavia

They leave
without seeing the fireflies
blinking
in my garden
without even remembering
the lies
cocoon inside which
we became chrysalises.

Claudia Pozzana
Bologna, 11 November 1990

Two Rustled Up And Found Again Poems[41]

Nests on the treetops
lonely among tangled branches
dry or nearly bare
by now stripped
in sulfurizing steam
boils the ancient rain
on the Roman tub
volcanic saturnine

I smile at whomever looks unavoidably
saddened
frowny behind the debris
of the trite almost powerfully distorted
treacherous momentum, they say
perhaps only the ancestral need of another
drowsy sweet softened smile

Claudia Pozzana
Saturnia, 21 November 2000. Bologna 13 October 2002

Aerial View of Kunlun Mountains[42]

And the sun will go down golden
Over these zebra-coloured hills,
The darkened precipices, snow-capped rills,
Layers of mist and clouds enfolding

Hewn granite, jagged basalt, glacial ice
Shining like halos in the sun
On mountain-tops whence rivers run
From the inception of their course.

The sun will set in streams of gold
Bathing the mountains in its light
Until soft shadows of the night
Envelop them in curtains cold.

Joanna Radwańska-Williams
9 June 2017
@ flight from Guangdong to Urumqi, China

Aubade in May[43]

Morning winks,
peeling back
the pinking skin of
dawn's

half-strewn fruit
on a great cerulean
      plate.
What could taste
      sweeter?
Revived at five
a.m., crakes cry

Wake! wake! Wake!
as we
jerk off migrating
bedding.

Birches quake with
anticipation—
a fox's wedding
creates
light, sating my
naked skin
with a fragrance of
apricot.

Steller's Jays greet
their mates
with blue, ear-ache
shrieks

screeching like
stable-gates.

Apus Apus race in
radiant air,
chasing each
other's tails
while you lazily
claim mine.

I rise at daybreak,
the shy finger
of Spring sun in my
eye

and kiss the smiling
face
of a sudden bliss:
happiness.
Whitecaps tease the
weighty lake,
while the graceful,
shining day

licks the gleaming
rim
of my teacup,
saying:

—*People! Age will
Sneak-up on you
anyway.
Shake your inner
child awake—
and come out to
play!*

kerry rawlinson

Echinacea Making Moonlight[44]

You were born through revision,
   not meant to be the serene mountain, companioning
   a gentle river guiding a boat downstream.

You gestated for three months, awaiting
   more complex brush strokes to pattern
   your life's journey.

Mountain peak longed to be the cone
   of your flowering;
     calligraphic language found your form of feeling

quickly, your twin flowered to companion you—
   your cone-faces upturning forever to admire
   an invisible moon.

I like the language! enjoyed Wang Gong-yi,
   How entered the moonlight? wondered the artist.
   Yes, I see it! professed peers.

Did you really paint that? Julia humoured my
     incredulity—
   even after "Echinacea Under Moonlight" had
     kindled
   Shenzhen Fine Arts Museum heart-minds.

Facing Trinity Episcopal Cathedral eyes,
   your lambency floated
     in the eye of an admirer, who felt

   your life force and brought you home
      to his New Mexico Buddhist monastery where
         you make magic in the foyer, inviting

each true contemplative to drink
   the silver yin moon to guide
      the way to new floating worlds—just down stream.

M. Ann Reed

Fire under Water[45]

How tender can
we bear to be?

Delicate Japanese
Maple leaves cup
rain in open hearts,
each drop cups sun, blinks

light, blinks stars, until
the green feathered universe beholds
what it means

to be rain cupped
in fire's chrysalis, harbouring
a new kind of wing,

and rain dreams
forest days among green synaptic
vibrations of sun.

M. Ann Reed

Following the Life Force[46]

Paint this peony, invites Wang Gongyi.
  No, I can't.
    Yes, you can. Learn to paint from life.

The peony's infinitely unfurling
  coastline of repeating waves receding
    into tinctures of darker to darkest pink, had lost

fullest poise—
  that *momentary stay*
    against confusion.*

Why did my hand refuse my eyes, attuning
  to musical coastlines?
    Keep it. Look again—next year.

By morning my hand understands
  (without thought or eyes) intricately felt gestures
    of peony coastlines.

Peony after peony quickly marries
  hand, gesture, paper, brush and ink, happy
    to live through art.

In her accordion book of hours,
  last evening's peony and children debut,
    gravid in black, charcoal, grey, pale grey and white
      petalage.

Yet her story remains half-told.
  On her birthday, I see what she had impressed—
    simultaneous birth, growth, maturation,

decline, death and the constellating moment
   of regeneration and rebirth—
     what plant cells teach botanists peering

through high-powered electron-microscopes—
   what botanist-poet Emily Dickinson directly knew
   and understood.

Muse of mystery, icon of life force,
   this peony had transmitted
     from her deep reveries

a force of increasing potentials told
   by each wave of coastline (hidden from dying
   thoughts and eyes) born of Dream.

M. Ann Reed

---

* From Robert Frost's poem, 'Directive'.

Today[47]

Today my joy
is a stringed instrument
a lightly touched arpeggio
a calamus laying on the sheet
a sinuous, sensual trace
secret, yet visible.
Today I choose my mother tongue
to put words
the one next to other
like roses in love.
Today I woke up
fullfilled by what I have
by the coffee that awaits me
by the echo of a flute
and I give thanks.

Angelo Rizzi

OF WORDS AND KEYS
Memory, Future and Everyday Lies

Voices in my head

I had a grandma
who first was a nun
and then lived in a cave.
I think I know that, at some point
between these two things,
she started to say—because she believed it—
that you do not bargain with the heart.
Or to believe it because she said it.
Hearts pump,
they push and push
up to the tip of your hands,
until they wake them up, naked like keys;
but you do not ask them what they open, what they close.
It's better to leave them counting,
the hands;
that's why they have fingers.
The ass has other things,
but don't ask it to count your money,
that's what my grandma used to say—
or maybe never said but I heard it—
you do not bargain with the voices in your head.

Why didn't you come to the funeral
I would not do this to my worst enemy
Give me back the keys
I can't marry you
Why did you tell him
Why didn't you tell him
I swear it was
I swear it wasn't
You were a son of a bitch.

You are a son of a bitch.

I had a grandma
who first was a nun
and then lived in a cave.
I know that, at some point
between these two things,
she was a refugee,
I was told
I wasn't told
Give me back the keys
Why didn't you come to the funeral.

José Manuel Sevilla

OF WORDS AND KEYS
Memory, Future and Everyday Lies

Silence is not sad[48]

Silence is not sad.
Silent movies are.
A bed is also sad.
That's why I was not born on a bed:
my mother gave birth to me standing up, alone,
gripping a window
and holding me with her legs.
Legs are not sad,
not those of a woman.

The army is sad.
There they didn't teach me how to drink,
of that I knew a fucking lot.
But I learned how to sleep on the floor,
march, slip away with the gipsy girls, all that;
not much, what military life back then could give.
Writing letters.
I got a postcard from my cousin Belen,
the one with a glass eye.
She killed herself in a motorbike accident.
The postcard was all black of course, no words.
When you die you become illiterate again.
Imagine, to go back to study all those school books,
with the drawing of the devil speaking at your ear;
so easy to become a sinner.
One of our neighbours in Jerusalem Street was a
sinner—as if taken out from our books, shorter
though—he only smoked when playing the piano
and his wife was a drunk;
those two were not friends with words;
losing a war didn't favour them too much.

I had lost it too, but that was long before I was born.
It's a long silent movie
before somebody gives birth to you.

José Manuel Sevilla

OF WORDS AND KEYS
Memory, Future and Everyday Lies

Soul Cleaning

They found not much, the thieves
who burgled our future:
some friendship in cash, a few hopes
that my mother had left me;
but all the words were in a mess—
everything we were supposed to say,
in the years to come,
scrambled on the floor, on the bed, in the kitchen,
the sentences in our wardrobes thrown everywhere,
as if a typhoon had passed.

In the kids' room we found
my elder daughter's only prayer to the Lord:
"I follow this diet with joy,
I am a lighter burden to You,"
next to the Walter White quote
that we kept in the safe—
it's not a grandmother's jewel,
but it has sentimental value
and it's been so useful to me—
"There must exist certain words in a specific order
that could explain all of this,
but I just can't ever seem to find them".[49]

All over the place were the bad words,
the moans, the screams—
I like them; bad as they are, they also clean,
as, in the old times, heretics were forced
to swallow red-hot iron, in what was called
Soul Cleaning.

How wrong have people always been, wanting
to go to heaven.

When I stumbled into, "Rome does not pay traitors", [50]
I looked around once more.
What did the burglars really expect to find
in our future?
Rome always pays traitors.

José Manuel Sevilla

OF WORDS AND KEYS
Memory, Future and Everyday Lies

Keys

The man who killed me came zigzagging
in the big truck through Rage Street.
It was my turn.
Shit, this life gets pregnant with unwanted pregnancies
every other day—well, that's why, in our family,
we all carried our keys
to the Kingdom of Heaven
with us, all the time.
You never know.

At home they made us fear many things—
like bathing before two hours after we accepted
candies from strangers—
But, losing those keys!
We could lose friendship, direction, time, the match,
hope,
the north, faith, virginity, memory, shame, respect,
temper,
even lose reflection in the mirror
and feed only on blood.
But not the damned keys.

Luckily, it was already Sunday morning.
During the years I lived with my family,
Sundays at 9 o'clock was the time to open the
windows and let the smell of fish go;
and at 10, to let the words that were like arrows go;
when, after the rice and siesta, it was time to learn
how to make snowmen;
because you never know.

I used to think with nostalgia of the wolves
who raised me,
of how today we would enjoy learning
all this unknown wickedness
coming from Saudi Arabia and the USA;
but my mother was quite strict;
she had not left her house to drag me along out of the
jungle, still wearing her apron,
to, you know.

I almost don't smell of a living man anymore,
the lines on my hands are like last month's newspaper.

It's about time to stop floating
on my back with the others,
as if Rage Street was a crowded swimming pool,
and grab the bag of El Corte Ingles
in which I have my tunic,
for the opening of the Red Sea,
because, you never know.

But what really nobody knows
is
that I also have a hidden set of keys
to the Kingdom of Wolves.

My heart still lives in the jungle,
believing that the war is not over.

José Manuel Sevilla

Encounter[51]
at a poetry workshop

Across the table our eyes were tied
in a speck of time as if by some ancient cord
your dark eyes released for a moment
from the words you were reading...
mine giving reply.

Old or young we are not immune
from a certain look that opens us
that moves through an inner wall
like seepage between layered limestone
tuned in a northern springtime.

You have held me in your eyes
—almost that is enough—
though yearning thighs ache for more...
I long to break commandments
to fly, to swim into surprise.

You are too old an inner voice chides
your face has wrinkles
when you bend down
the years tell their stories
no matter what the heart decries.

Perhaps we touched across a great divide
a table's width eclipsing years
maybe a century ago
when we were lovers...
I wander in the long shadows.

Allegra Silberstein

Happiness and I[52]
tongue-in-cheek free verse laced with philosophy

Happiness and I will be friends, by and by.
I run after happiness and she thinks it's a game—
she touches my hand, she calls out my name,
she giggles and runs—then I hunt once again.
I love her, I love her, I love her a lot,
but oh, my goodness, what a cheek she's got!
I spend my life desperate to catch her
as she taunts and she flaunts
and makes sure that I watch her…
then off she goes, but where?
Here? There? Nobody knows.
All I know for sure
(and there seems precious little cure)
is I'm doomed to endure the throes of heart-sinking
(tears wet and blinking
from my nose), oh, yes, so it goes,
from that nose to the end of my toes!
"Come back happiness! Come back!" I plead,
"If you tease me too long, my heart starts to bleed!
I need to find you and hold you and feel you are mine,
stay with me please, oh stay just this time!"
So happiness grins, and flings me a kiss.
I laugh from pure joy and bottle her bliss.
But she wriggles and squirms, then takes it in turns
to annoy and provoke and smile or just poke,
so I set her free and just let her be.
My greatest, greatest, *greatest* content
is when she cuddles me sweetly
and tells me it's meant:
meant for us two to have nothing to do,
but bask in the sun and simply have fun,
Or else find a way to make *other* folks play.

Huh?
I ask her what she means, and she says we're a team.
Happiness grows when love overflows.
Happiness is not finite but infinite;
everyone's friend, if in the end,
we are generous, open, kind and not greedy,
happiness happens, it does,
oh indeedy!
Joy floats in bubbles and wafts away troubles,
delight, as our right, lights up the night,
for happiness shared...
is happiness squared.
If you hold my hand," she says, "Don't let it go,
but join hands with others so we all overflow,
and *always* take note, take *note* of me
lest I somehow escape or just simply flee.
Don't look for riches—riches aren't me;
when you share me I'm yours,
When you give me I double, give me and give me...
and smile on the double!
So I do and I did, and happiness stays,
I share her with joy—
'cos I've learnt all her ways!

Hayley Ann Solomon

Have I Found You, Utopia?[53]

Have I found you, Utopia,
in the soft greens and blues of this country,
lush with living and soaked with forgiving?

Have I found you in the hard crevices of earth,
softened by wind power and plantings,
rain and reasoned method?

Or in the sheep that dapple the landscape
like echoes of summer sky,
puddles of cotton cloud grazing assiduously,
but all there, each and every one,
because of fence lines and labour,
cell biology and genetics,
  man and technology, working in unison?

Have I found you
because we are a society with a voice and a heart?
We might not agree, but we can agree to disagree,
for there are more truths than just our own,
and a veritable rainbow of perceptions
we can imbue with respect.

Utopia is a prism,
multifaceted,
casting light on such a multiplicity of perspectives
that we are illuminated and challenged,
not drowned and despairing.

If the refracted light shines blue to our vivid pink,
green to our vermillion,
we can argue for change: in freedom.
Yes, we can subtly alter the arc of light through
persuasion, logic,
the application of sound principles.

Sometimes the light will refract,
dappling the landscape,
allowing our own perceptions and conceptions
to shade a little, or transform,
or find an epiphanal colour of brilliance
that is both congruent and congruous,
a glow that is as gloried as it is glorious.

Here there are no profoundly rich,
but then, there is no poverty of soul.
And with no poverty of soul, we are profoundly rich.
Utopia, robed in sashes of silk and a sturdy apron,
smiles.

'What shall I call you? I ask.

"Call me happiness," she replies.

Hayley Ann Solomon

How do I love you? [54]
An Acrostic of Happiness

H ow do I love you?
A day can't measure the hours, nor a
p iano play the multiplicity of tones
p lucking pizzicato on my heartstrings. They thrum in perpetual
i nvitation, meandering through my thoughts in chords that hum of you, a
n exus of vibrato so subtly poetic, so lyrically resonant, that it
e quilibrates to your very voice. I dream your depths, bass-deep with bliss.
S uch is my love, pitched not to time, but to your harmonies. My feelings flutter,
s ynchronous with the very best of myself. A-hum, on high, they resonate
                                    happiness

Hayley Ann Solomon

Four Walls[55]

Somebody is giving birth in the room next door.
Nine months is up, it's time for the big arrival.

The rest of us are pregnant with the future—
Pregnant with possibilities
Each one opening out—a door to walk though, an invitation.

The midwife arrives bearing oxygen
Which is not needed
More pushing is done,
The umbilical cord is cut—time's up,
Three kilos of perfection is delivered.

Laura Solomon

Trestle

Trestle is the place memory must pass
Train, a configuration of high-density steel and flesh
Swoops in, backtracking on the railway like a wound
Minute by minute, persuading the mountain to retreat

How does the trestle make life rough, the river more
        rapid?
Whenever someone asks, lost people gush out like
low notes of a cello

They converse with shadows
in a dark language, but they can never
portray it under the sun
Memory is a horse on the string
Flickers where they haven't arrived

Tolerance is vague
Yet those resentments take the shape of
A secret pastureland or
clumps of grey clouds yet to be dispersed
Void guards them, using time to console them

Yet the design of the trestle lies in its postures
So many standpoints…floors…
and the illusion of time, a secret dimension bursting
        open and overlapping
the moment when a train hits the bones
we approach, they resist, recede, shut
Everything is so irreconcilable
The injured space has grown old
Yet the track of time is still etched
in the sky above the trestle though it is blue and
        cloudless.

Thus, revenge is cleansed
Thus, forgiveness is meaningless.

Dong Sun

Stay Away From MY Tree House[56]

Little one, it looks inviting, doesn't it,
a house nestled in an old oak tree?
It's far from homey.

It came with this house I bought ten years ago.
I don't know how long it's been there,
wooden ladder rickety, perhaps unstable.

If you manage to get to the top,
who knows if the structure would bear weight?
Like the cradled baby in the treetop,
you and the house could tumble down, down, down,
land on the ground all broken.

The ambulance would take you away.
Wearing a body cast from head to toe,
you'd spend weeks, months in the hospital.
Unable to do anything
but lie there and watch television,
you'd long to be outside with your friends.
Dora the Explorer would get old after a while.

Your parents would sue me.
I'd have to sell my house
in order to pay your hospital bill,
move to a senior apartment complex,
where I would no longer enjoy my own back yard,

so you'd better not climb into my tree house
if you know what's good for both of us.

Abbie Taylor

Happiness on the Beach[57]
as seen at Pui O, Lantau Island, Hong Kong

Steaming hot is the sunlight
The beach receives the shine of the sea
Hills are blue
Wild buffaloes roam the beach
Hardly noticed by the crowd
Dusk comes
Little by little.
A young lady reads on
Types tiny messages
On her telephone.
A buffalo is behind her.
Just sniffing her bags
Ah! Food different from grass!
A bather warns her of impending danger.
She jumps on her feet, startled,
But then she begins filming
the buffalo searching her bags
And she laughs and lets it go.
The joy of sharing some food with a wild buffalo!
Laughter fills her heart
Laughter fills the space around.
Soon the moon will come
Dispersing the crowds
Guiding the buffaloes to their forests
Laughter—filmed—will last.

Luisa Ternau

In Fear of Dusk

This is the hour that judges you
That makes you fear
Looking at your own self in the mirror.
The dust and dirt of the day
Cover your face, your body
In sticky layers.
And yet the heart beats on.
The day is vanishing over the sky-scrapers' tops.
Street lights are being lit
Even offices seem to glow
in the impending dusk.
Red, green, red, green, red, green
The raging traffic is controlled.
On your pocket mirror
Your dreamy face covets
Colourful butterflies
Embroidered on clothes
Behind the shop-window.
They even seem to hover
Taking your thoughts
Over the flaming clouds
Where Cupid is dozing off
An uncast arrow loose
On his lap.
The heart expands
In total readiness to receive it.
Pinging devices show messages from
Work, advertisements, more work
Darkness after dusk is
Only for the distant horizon
Where layers of dust and dirt
Matter no more.

Luisa Ternau

Metropolitan Happiness

Sitting on the bench
Around me I hear
Footsteps in the wind
Mingled with voices
Not so faraway
Colourful lights dancing out of the walls
Hoping to reach the stars
Or dashed to the ground
Like arrows cast from outer space.
After all, even a metropolis
Is not large enough
To contain all my dreams, thoughts
Reasonings, hesitations, emotions.

Sitting on the bench
Yet where am I?
My weight is like a feather
Following the neon pink light
Up and up and up
Well over the skyscrapers' tops
Reaching high over the airplanes
An angel smiles at me
Touching me, holding me tight
With strong arms

Suddenly, fearing to fall,
I cling to the angel
And oh! I see the tree before me
The street overcrowded with footsteps
And their owners' voices
I am just sitting on the bench
Lights dancing by
Their vivid colours patting
My face, my dress, my body
With quick caresses

People walk by
They don't know I soared
So high into the sky
To touch the most beautiful being
With wings light and strong
With muscular arms
To clutch my happiness
Never to give it back to me!

Luisa Ternau

Party Night

Sparkling is the chit chat, oh so adorable!
A successful party
Is a happy circumstance indeed
To be cherished
At least for the sheer
Suspension
from all the rest
In life
And still, this happiness is life too

Luisa Ternau

Viet Nam Journey: Ha Noi Alley[58]

Heated exhaust from
scooters and cars
the odors of
sewage and ladies' perfume
and grilling meat
and hanging poultry
and tropical fruit
merge and embrace
the narrow, crowded walk way.

A short-haired young mother
spoon feeds her child
its first solid food
as the grandmother
shouts encouragement
and praise
from across the path
her cries of joy
punctuated with
hands clapping.

Further on
spit-roasted dogs
are stacked in small mounds
on waist-high metal counters
as if they
were an offering to
a frowning deity.

Next door
in the far corner incense
burns and its smoke
wanders among
the flowers and gifts
at the ancestors' shrine.

On a thread-bare sofa
a young man and woman
kiss and caress
each other silently
their breathing ghost-like
not wanting to draw attention
from card-playing parents
or departed grandparents.

Across the way
two boys
watch cartoons on a
flickering small screen TV
the volume turned low
their laughter muffled
as they become super heroes
and play-fight
with worn pillows.

The voices from the homes
hover in the alley
and are dampened
in the cloudy humidity
the sounds of unnoticed lives
on the cobbled stones.

Edward Tiesse

Viet Nam Journey: The Jade Pagoda

Crowded on the sidewalk
nearly spilling into the street,
a weathered woman
of indeterminate age
begging us to buy
turtles or
goldfish or
caged sparrows
to set free
on the grounds of the pagoda.

Incense hangs heavy in
the dank afternoon air
as carved sentinels
swords in scabbards
loom over us and
stare into centuries past
where ancestors walk
down silent corridors and move
in the rustling of leaves and
the weeping of rain.

A white and tabby spotted cat
pads noiselessly across
blood-stained coloured roof tiles
a still twitching mouse
seized solidly in its jaws
not yet ready to join
his grandfather.

Edward Tiesse

Satan's Taxing Times[59]

'Tis time we all should understand
that behind every evil
there is the dark, sinister hand
of Satan, the eternal devil.

When Satan sees the population
on earth having lots of fun,
with food, wine and copulation,
he fears Hell will come undone.

So he contacts his covert agents
and expounds on his inner frustration,
with directives to Prime Ministers and Presidents
to escalate the rate of taxation.

For he knows when taxes rise
people feel depressed and unwell
and are lured by the tempting prize
of the tax-free pleasures of Hell.

So no matter what games you play,
whether cricket, chess or hockey,
unless you go to Hell for the day
Satan's hand will be picking your pockie!

Roger Uren

Happiness Entries in My Diary[60]

Happiness on 10 May 2017
It is such bliss to sit in the sunshine- filled corner of
the room
And to just feel the warmth on your face
And do nothing
Half-dazed, half-awake.
Just being.

Happiness on 11 May 2017
To witness serenity personified, the Lantau Buddha
to melt in the yellowness of the lotus in the pond
to follow the calm trail of the Wisdom Path
to warm the heart with vermicelli in the Monastery
food –joint
Just being.

Happiness on 16 May 2017
The waves come dashing, breathless to reach the shore
Lined up in quick succession
Breathless to dissolve in the vastness
The pattern repetitive, yet so beautiful each time.
Just being.

Happiness on 20 May 2017
The wayside flower, fragile and simple
Stand and look at it or just pass by
It doesn't care, it doesn't demand attention
A quiet, tiny, joyous life singing the song of subtle
existence.
Just being.

Happiness on 1 June 2017
That old Peepul tree in the courtyard has burst into
new colours
Sparkling its tender red leaves in the sunlight
Before they decide to go green
The squirrels scamper up and down.
Just being.

No Happiness Days
Plumbing, ironing, driving and cooking
Sulking, expecting, cursing and squabbling
Days without little pleasures
Days without the quietude of nature
Days without just being.

Deepa Vanjani

Being Lost Along The Way[61]

Going somewhere, finding nowhere,
Being lost along the way,
Round in circles, forth and back,
Sum total of my working day.

What's the point in going somewhere,
If there's nowhere at the end?
Going round and round in circles,
Need a mentor, or a friend

Who will show me how to get there,
No more losses on the way.
Straight for goals, not going backwards,
Satisfaction on a working day.

Joyce Walker

Elegy For My Father[62]

Your path progressed
from doctor to doctors,
from pills to injections,
from driving
to being chauffeured.
Your walk went from cane
to canes, from walkers
to nothing, your last trip
a gurney, the final journey
wrapped within a sheet.

Since we buried you,
the slowness of your shuffle
no longer matters.
Since we buried you,
that time-wasting drive
you asked me to make
across town
for one carton of cotton balls,
the *only* ones you wanted?
I wish I could do it again.

But now,
I would lean into
your every word.
I would savor
every trivial trip
and shuffled step.

I would be patient,
knowing
this
is everything.

Bruce Wasserman

Gratitude[63]

Let's be the first to say "hello"
Whoever we are, wherever we go.
A simple phrase like, "I thank you,"
Will show goodwill in what we do.
And often it's our silly smile
That makes our chores seem worthwhile.
Gratitude expressed in any form
Carries us through rain and storm.
We might be angry in different ways.
But think good thoughts! Anger fades!
Our happiness is just a bore
Without gratitude at its core.
To be grateful from the heart
Will let happiness play its part.

Elizabeth Libby Wong

An Angel's Kiss[64]

Hearing whispers soft as feathers,
Still and graceful as he smiled.
With the resilience of a warrior,
In the body of a child.
We fight this thing together,
By the grace of God prevail.
I wish I had his faith and strength,
Cancer's storm of fear assail.
My body's growing tired,
And my baby boy's at rest
I shut my eyes for a little while,
My hopes and prayers abreast.
Then I heard the sound of harmony,
A thousand voices singing true.
In the dim lit room, they sang a tune,
A dream of truth I knew.
I sat up and rubbed my eyes,
Then laughed among the tears.
But I heard the echo of his name,
As wistful winds within my ears.
Then I saw the shadows
As the Angels left my sight.
And set my heart a pounding,
And let my Prayers take flight.
I know that every wish was heard,
And I know that someone cares.
After all it's promised in his word,
That we'll meet Angels unaware.
And as I checked my son asleep,
Wondering if my dream's amiss
I saw stardust on his forehead,
In the shape of an Angel's kiss

Thomas Young

Interlude[65]

At first thaw
We will plunge our limbs into the shards,
Flutter madly
And meet amid the tea-green weeds.

Until then
This lake is a wine-white sea between us.

On opposite shores we stand and wait,
Eyes skyward,
Silent as sea glass.

Sending messages in bottles
Flung from slumbering beaches,
Cracking as they fall.
Splinters in a hundred directions,
Words lost to the wind.

For now
Dream of winter's passing
When we shall meet once more,
And the cranes return,
At first thaw.

Sally Younger

POETS' BRIEF BIOGRAPHIES
(provided by the poets)

VINITA AGRAWAL is a Mumbai-based, award winning poet and writer, the author of three books of poetry. She is Editor of Womaninc.com, an online platform that addresses gender issues. Recipient of the Gayatri GaMarsh Memorial Award for Literary Excellence, USA, 2015, her poems have appeared in *Asiancha*, *Constellations*, *The Fox Chase Review*, *Pea River Journal*, *Open Road Review*, *Stockholm Literary Review*, *Poetry Pacific*, *Mithila Review* and other journals. She was nominated for the Best of the Net Awards in 2011. She was awarded first prize in the Wordweavers Contest 2014, a commendation prize in the All India Poetry Competition 2014 and won the 2014 Hour of Writes Contest three times. Her poems have found a place in several anthologies. She contributes a monthly column on Asian Poets on the literary blog of the Hamline University, Saint Paul, USA. She has read at SAARC events, at the U.S. Consulate, at Delhi Poetree and at Cappucino Readings, Mumbai. She has been featured in a transatlantic poetry broadcast.

INDRAN AMIRTHANAYAGAM has published eleven poetry collections to date, including *The Elephants of Reckoning* which won the 1994 Paterson Poetry Prize in the United States. He writes in French, Spanish, Haitian Creole and Portuguese in addition to English. His latest book in English, *Uncivil War*, is a history in poetry of the Sri Lankan Civil War.

LIAM BLACKFORD is an Australian lawyer living and working in Hong Kong.

MARÍA ELENA BLANCO (Havana, Cuba) is a poet, essayist and translator who writes predominantly in her native Spanish. Having spent a good part of her formative years in New York, she translates her own poetry into English and has also developed her own English poetic voice in a style quite distinguishable from her Spanish one.

She has taught French literature and language and worked for the United Nations as translator/reviser, presently on a freelance basis. She is a frequent participant in international literary events and a member of Labyrinth, the Association of English-Speaking Poets in Vienna. Her published work includes poetry collections *Posesión por pérdida* (Sevilla and Santiago, Chile, 1990), *Corazón sobre la tierra / tierra en los Ojos* (Cuba, 1998), Alquímica memoria (Madrid, 2001), *Mitologuías* (Madrid, 2001), *danubiomediterráneo /mittelmeerdonau* (Vienna, 2005, Spanish-German), *El amor incontable* (Madrid, 2008), *Havanity / Habanidad* (Miami, 2010, English-Spanish), *Escrito en lenguas* (Chile, 2015), *Sobresalto al vacío* (Chile, 2015) and *Botín* (Leiden, 2016), as well as a book of literary criticism, *Asedios al texto literario* (Madrid, 1999), and a volume of critical essays on Cuban culture and politics, *Devoraciones. Ensayos de período especial* (Leiden, 2016). She has also published Spanish translations of French and Austrian poets, among others. She divides her time between her home in Vienna (Austria), Chile, and the Andalusian countryside.

GIORGIO BOLLA is a Venetian poet and essayist, fifty-nine years old. His poetry is symbolist, nearly automatic. He has published twelve poetic sylloges (some translated into Spanish) and a philosophic essay on the metaphor (in English). He has won numerous national and international prizes of poetry.

EVA BROWN writes under the pen name, PANNI PALÁSTI, her maiden name. She was born in Budapest and educated there. She fled to the United States after the defeat of the Hungarian Revolution in 1956. She lived in New York, Ohio and California, where she taught English and worked as a feature writer for a daily newspaper. She sailed with her husband and small son to New Zealand in 1973 and settled in the Bay of Islands, where she started and edited the *Russell Review* and founded the Russell Writers Workshop. She moved to Nelson in 2002, where she joined the Nelson Live Poets group. Her publications include a volume of poems, *Taxi! Taxi!*, a memoir of her childhood in war-torn Budapest, *Budapest Girl: An Immigrant Confronts the Past*. Her poetry has also been published on the CDs, *Born in Budapest* and *Love and War in the Yurt*, with jazz accompaniment by Gabor Tolnay and Simon Williams. She is currently working on another volume of poems.

PAOLA CARONNI is from Milan, Italy and has been living in Asia since 1995. She is a freelance translator, tutor of the Italian language, writer and poet. She recently completed an MFA in Creative Writing at the University of Hong Kong and holds an MA in English Language and Literature from the University of Milan. Paola's poems have been included in two poetry anthologies, *Desde Hong Kong: Poets in Conversation with Octavio Paz* and *Quixotica: Poems East of La Mancha* and have appeared in *Cha, an Asian Literary Journal*. Since 2014, she has been a regular contributor to the cultural platform 'Beyond Thirty-nine', where she publishes articles, fiction and poetry.

JOSIE CHAMBERS has worked as an organisational consultant to a wide range of public sector organisations, including government departments and universities and as a senior manager in a UK university. She was awarded the MBE in the 2011 Queen's Birthday Honours for services to Higher Education. She now co-ordinates the work funded by a charity, which looks for, "approaches and initiatives which help young people, whatever their background, to live fulfilling and productive lives." Exploring the role of poetry in the 21st century, she looks for ways of using language simply and sparingly, whilst squeezing from few words a richer range of possibilities.

BENNY CHIA is the director and founder of a contemporary arts space that he has converted from a derelict ice depot (now a listed grade-1 heritage building). He has curated exhibitions with works by artists as wide-ranging as Frogking, Helmut Newton, Robert Rauschenberg, Wong Shun Kit and others. He has written scripts for stage productions choreographed and directed by

Kaitai Chan of One Extra Dance Company, and Fisher King of Sydney Theatre Company; and site-specific dramatisations with Tang Shu Wing. His short stories have been published in magazines and newspapers. With poetry-writing, he is a newcomer. This is the second time he has entered a poetry competition; the first time he was at university and his poem won him a prize from Radio Television Hong Kong the host of the competition.

PSYCHE CHONG, a lawyer and amateur artist, was born in Hong Kong. Art for Psyche is an intrinsic expression. In their daily lives, people need to express themselves, they need to talk and be understood. Although self-expression is very personal, it is also universal. Art and culture cannot be separated from philosophy. From a philosophical point of view, the transformation of feelings into form or matter is a metaphysical necessity subject to our intrinsic limitation, no matter whether it is western or eastern. It was in this spirit that, in December 2007, Psyche started to paint. Her debut solo exhibition was held in 2008, and since then she has held fifteen solo, dual and group art exhibitions. In the last two years, Psyche has also started to sculpt and write both in Chinese and English so to transform her passion into different representations.

TERESA N. F. CHU grew up with dogs as family pets, and since childhood, has always looked upon them as part of the family; indeed as life coaches.

WILLIAM LEO COAKLEY has been published in the *Paris Review*, *London Magazine*, the *Nation*, *New American Review*, *Poetry Review* (London), and magazines, newspapers, and anthologies in America, England, Ireland, and Mexico. Since being selected for the Discovery series at the New York Poetry Center, he has read his poems at colleges, art galleries, museums, and pubs, in the *Day without Art* programmes, and on television and radio, as well as at Barnes & Noble Union Square in New York as part of the W. B. Yeats Society 2011 and 2015 Annual Awards ceremonies. His 'Horses Burning' won a Sotheby's

International Poetry Competition Prize and his translation of a Constantine Cavafy poem won the 2013 Der Hovanessian Prize of the New England Poetry Club. He also was on the longlist for the 2015 Montreal Prize and a finalist for the Aesthetica Creative Writing Award 2015 in England. Born in Boston but now also an Irish citizen, he is publisher of Helikon Press.

NICK COMPTON is a writer, traveller and poet. He has been published in both Canada and the UK. Alex Culotta PhD has described his style as, "bold yet unassuming, a refreshing voice in a handful of powerful stanzas". In addition to writing for the *Huffington Post*, he teaches poetry in workshops and lectures and is a member of the Rhyme and Reason Poetry Collective. A musketeer at heart, you can normally spot him with a trusty cup of tea by his side.

LUCY DUGGAN is a writer and translator based in rural Brandenburg, eastern Germany. She recently finished a PhD in Czech and German literature at Oxford University. Currently, she is working on a queer family saga set in a ruined manor house. She is the author of *Tendrils* (Peer Press, 2014), a novel about long-lost enemies. Her miniature stories can be found at www.tinystori.es.

LUKE ENGLISH is a new writer, nineteen years old at the time of entering for the Proverse Poetry Prize and born in Charlestown, Rhode Island, the smallest town in the smallest state. He has been lucky enough to see the world, traveling with his mother. When he was seventeen, he spent a year aboard the Dutch sail training vessel, *Gulden Leeuw*, sailing the world and writing about what he saw. It was on board that he found a passion for writing, mostly about the sea. It was a piece he wrote on the purple mornings of the Mid-Atlantic that served as his college essay and got him into the university of his dreams that he currently attends, Quest University Canada.

HASAN ERKEK is a poet, playwright and a professor of drama. He has been awarded more than twenty national and international prizes. He has published twenty-five artistic and academic books in thirteen different countries.

PETER FRECKLETON lives in Melbourne, Australia. For as long as he can recall he has loved language, which led him to Paris where he earned a doctorate in Linguistics. He is a translator and attorney. As a barrister for thirty years, he has been involved in many cases, some humourous, others traumatic. Told as a six-year-old that he could, "earn a living" with his pen, he took it as promise, like a gypsy fortune-teller's scrying. Since then he has circled around it, working in academia and the law, writing papers and court submissions. Lately he has attempted a more lyrical form.

SANDRA GIBBONS started her life's journey in 1954 in government housing located in a working-class suburb of Sydney, Australia. With her five siblings, the harmony and joy of her upbringing was forever disrupted as a result of her mother's episodes of anxiety and depression. For much of her life, Sandra did not understand the chaos around her.

As she has ventured through her academic studies in politics and law, her friendships and relationships, her work in intellectual property law, her relocation to Hong Kong in 1995 and, as the first approved single parent by Hong Kong Social Services, the adoption of her darling daughter now twenty years old, she has sought to make sense of her past and to understand her own struggles with anxiety and depression.

Sandra dedicates her writing to those who live with challenges of the psyche and seeks to bring an understanding to those who have never experienced the internal darkness. She thanks everyone who has accepted her for who she is.

ELIZABETH HESTER GROBLER is originally from South Africa, where she obtained her Primary Education Degree, BEd Honours Degree in Learning Support, Guidance and Counselling as well as a B.A. Honours

Degree in Afrikaans, Dutch & Flemish Literature from the University of Pretoria. She taught African English as a Second Language (ESL) students in South Africa. She also wrote, directed and produced plays for her school's drama troupe. In 2006 she moved to South Korea where she wrote curricula, taught English (mainly with drama and music as subject matter) and wrote and directed educational plays for children's theatre. She arrived in Hong Kong in 2010 and has been a member of the Society of Children's Book Writers and Illustrators (SCBWI) and the Hong Kong Women in Publishing Society (HKWIPS) since then. Several of her poems and short stories have been published in the HKWIPS annual anthology, *Imprint*. Elizabeth has been teaching at a primary school on Hong Kong Island for the past seven years where she enjoys developing curricula as well as writing and directing plays for the school's Campus TV and stage productions.

KATE HAWKINS is an actor, TV presenter, voice over artist, poet, scriptwriter and editor living in Hong Kong, a city where she also spent part of her childhood. She has written scripts for television and is currently writing her first feature film. She co-edited two Hong Kong Writers Circle (HKWC) anthologies, *Another Hong Kong* and *Hong Kong Gothic* and has also been published in HKWC anthologies. She holds a degree in Creative Writing from Queensland University of Technology in Brisbane, Australia and has been writing for as long as she can remember.

HENRIK HOEG is a Danish poet living in Hong Kong where he organizes and emcees Peel Street Poetry. His first collection *Irreverent Poems for Pretentious People* was published by Proverse Hong Kong in April, 2016. His poems have been published in such places as *Magma*, *East Lit*, *Time Out Magazine* and *Cha*.

VIKI HOLMES is a widely anthologised and prize-winning British poet and performer who began her writing career in Cardiff, Wales as part of the Happy Demon poetry collective. She has been living and writing in Hong Kong since 2005. Her poetry has appeared in literary magazines and anthologies in four continents, and has been translated into Chinese, Arabic and Uzbek. She is the author of *miss moon's class* (Chameleon Press, 2008), and co-editor of the anthology of world women's writing *Not A Muse* (Haven Books, 2009), which launched at literary festivals in Hong Kong and around the world. Her second collection of poetry, *Girls' Adventure Stories of Long Ago*, was published by Chameleon Press in 2017.

JANET JOYNER's poems have appeared in numerous magazines, among them, *American Athenaeum*, *The Cincinnati Review*, *The Comstock Review*, *Emrys Journal*, *Pembroke Magazine*, and *Main Street Rag*. Her prize winning poems are honoured in the 2011 Yearbook of the South Carolina Poetry Society, *Bay Leaves* of the North Carolina Poetry Council in 2010, 2011, and in *Flying South* in 2014, and 2015, as well as anthologized in *The Southern Poetry Anthology*, Volume VII: North Carolina; and *Second Spring 2016 Anthology*. Her first collection of poems, *Waterborne*, is the winner of the Holland Prize and was published in February 2016, by Logan House Press. Her short stories have appeared in *The Crescent Review*, *Flying South*, and *Second Spring Anthology* 2016. She is the translator of *Le Dieu désarmé* by Luc-François Dumas. She lives and writes in Winston-Salem, North Carolina, USA.

LYNDA MCKINNEY LAMBERT is the author of two books, *Concerti: Psalms for the Pilgrimage*, a book of poetry and short reflections from her travels in Europe each summer while teaching a course in drawing and writing to college students, and *Walking by Inner Vision: Stories & Poems*, a collection of sixteen poems and twenty-seven stories. She holds degrees in Fine Arts and English (BFA and MFA in Fine Arts; MA in English). She is an actively exhibiting visual artist of mixed media fiber art. She writes for a number of literary magazines.

MARGUS LATTIK aka Mathura is an Estonian poet and writer, author of eight collections of poetry and a short novel. He has won the Gustav Suits Poetry Award (2014) and the Virumaa Literary Award for the best historical novel of the year (2017).

SUSAN LAVENDER is a solicitor, actress, radio newsreader, member of Hong Kong Peel Street Poets and an actor member of Hong Kong Liars' League. She is a registered interpreter/translator of Italian/English at the Italian Consulate in Hong Kong and has worked as an advisor (English/Italian) for the Hong Kong Academy of Performing Arts. Anglo-Italian by birth, she is a former Vice President of the Italian Chamber of Commerce in Hong Kong & Macao. She likes languages. She is fluent in French having worked as an adjudicator in Quebec, Canada. She has learnt Rumanian and Chinese, having studied Mandarin in Beijing.

She studied acting at the Drama Studio, Ealing, UK, in the seventies and continues to perform in theatre, films, videos, voice-overs and story-telling events. Her work includes a BBC World Video on tourism on Hainan Island, a local Chinese martial arts film and theatre roles, such as the part of Mother Teresa in *The Last Days of Judas Iscariot*, a punk witch in Shakespeare's *Macbeth* and Rita in *Filumena* by Eduardo De Filippo. She started writing poetry in 2016 with the aim of one day completing an anthology of her poems.

LEE CHING YIN is a student in Hong Kong, a fan of European History, creative writing, and travelling. Her favourite book by far is Harper Lee's *To Kill a Mockingbird*. As a realist who is also fond of day-dreaming, Lee Ching Yin has always been fascinated by this novel, with its touch of childhood adventure mixed with grounded discussion on controversial issues. Throughout her teenage years, Ching Yin has been profoundly influenced by a vast encounter with traditional English literature and inspiring modern life-stories.

LEE Ho Cheung (Peter), Ed.D., is the founding editor of BALLOONS Lit. Journal. His second poetry chapbook "Something Celebrative and Immortal Under Another Birdless Sky" is forthcoming from Jamii Publishing. His work (poetry, short stories or photography) has appeared or is forthcoming in *Rattle*, **82 Review Magazine*, *Shearsman Magazine*, *Interpreter's House*, *The Writing Disorder*, *The Oddville Press*, and elsewhere. His poetry was shortlisted in Oxford Brookes University's International Poetry Competition (2016) and for the erbacce-prize for poetry (2017). He teaches English in Hong Kong. W: <www.ho-cheung.com>

DEREK LEI is Lei Chan Kit, from Macau. He's not really a writer but he writes almost everyday. He has a story and a poem printed in a local literary magazine that is free but nobody reads. He writes mostly in English, his second language, a language he has to constantly fight with, especially when the days are long and endless and the luck bad and without humour, but he thinks that's the best fight there is and he would write and write until he dies on a line that his mom would appreciate without asking him why.

LEUNG CHING NING is a Hong Kong native. She graduated from Hang Seng Management College with a B.A. in English. She is passionate about music, writing poetry and lately theatre as well. She started writing English poems in high school and grew fond of rhyming. She likes to explore new experiences in life and will keep trying until she fulfills her many dreams and goals, such as being a stage manager, a published poet/ writer and a musician or even a comedy actress. She is now an event management assistant who helps organizing indie band shows in Hong Kong.

LAWRENCE MALU is a poet, singer, film-maker and film-festival CEO.

MARTA MARKOSKA was born on 29 June 1981 in Skopje, Macedonia. She holds a Bachelor of General and Comparative Literature from the Blaze Koneski Faculty of Philology in Skopje, and a Master of Cultural Studies in Literature from the Institute of Macedonian Literature in Skopje and she is a member of the Writers' Association of Macedonia.

Her publications to date are: *Black Holes Within Us*, Second Edition, Macedonian-English translation (Todor Chalovski Award, 2015); *Black Holes Within Us*, poetry book (Beli Mugri Award, 2014); *Culture and Memory* (Book of Cultural Studies), Matica, 2014; A Discussion on Zen Buddhism: A Religious and Philosophical Transcendence Between Eastern and Western Thought, a scientific study (Matica, 2013); *Headfirst Toward the Heights*, poetry (2nd edition); *Headfirst Toward the Heights*, poetry (winner of the 2012 Aco Karamanov award); *Hyper Hypotheses*, a collection of essays (Institute of Macedonian Literature, 2011); *Whirlpool in Bethlehem*, a collection of stories (Templum, 2010); *All Tributaries Flow Into My Basin*, poetry (Templum, 2009).

Marta Markoska has been included in many anthologies and she is also an anthology-maker and author of the preface to, *Love Sailings Reefs* (an anthology of poems dedicated to Eros and Love), 2014.

Markoska has won the following awards: "Todor Calovski" (2015) for poetry, essays, critical and creative prose; "Nova Makedonija" (2015) for her short story 'Heights of Felix', "Beli Mugri" (2014) for her poetry book, *Black Holes Within Us*, "Aco Karamanov" (2012) for her poetry book, *Headfirst Toward The Heights*, and "Elektrolit" (2007) for best short story, 'What happens when you're reading Frazer'.

JACK MAYER is a Vermont writer and pediatrician. His was the first pediatric practice in Eastern Franklin County, on the Canadian border, where he began writing essays, poems and short stories about his practice and hiking Vermont's Long Trail. He was a country doctor for ten years, often bartering medical care for eggs, firewood, and knitted afghans. From 1987-1991 Dr. Mayer was a National Cancer Institute Fellow at Columbia University, researching the molecular biology of pediatric cancers. He established Rainbow Pediatrics in Middlebury, Vermont in 1991, where he continues to practice primary care pediatrics. He is an Instructor in Pediatrics at the University of Vermont School of Medicine and an adjunct faculty for pre-medical students at Middlebury College. He was a participant at the Bread Loaf Writers' Conference in 2003 and 2005 (fiction) and 2008 (poetry). His first non-fiction book is *Life In A Jar: The Irena Sendler Project*. His most recent book, *Before The Court Of Heaven*, is historical fiction and has received thirteen book awards.

MAYA MITOVA was born in the town of Blagoevgrad, Bulgaria and now lives in the town of Kresna in the neighbourhood of Blagoevgrad. She. graduated in Preschool education in 1990, and in Bulgarian philology in Blagoevgrad-Southwestern University in 1994. From 1994 up to the present she has worked as a teacher of Bulgarian Language and Literature in the "Father Paisii" Kresna, secondary school. Her books of poetry, *Drifter* (2003) and *Romantic Sax for Summer Passers-By* (2017), were published by the publishing house, "Zahari Stoyanov" (Sofia, Bulgaria).

She has won many poetry awards from national and international literary competitions, for example as follows.

In the sixth national competition for the most original character in a story or a poem by a modern Bulgarian author, "Irrelevant 2012", she was named, "Golden Irrelevant".

In the "Dora Gabe 2012" national award for young poets, she was awarded 1st prize by the Bulgarian Union of Writers, General Toshevo district.

She was named, "Albatros" for poetry, in Biela 2013 MONTENEGRO, awarded by the Literary Society, "Milutin Alempievich", of Frankfurt am Main in Germany.

In 2015, she won first prize in the XVI International Festival Melnik Poetry Evenings and also in the XV National Poetry Competition "Love ...".

She was Laureate of the III International Festival of Arts, "Morning Star", held in Bansko, Bulgaria, 2010.

Her poems have been translated into Serbian, Croatian, Macedonian, Romanian, English and German.

KAIT MOLLER was twenty-three years old at the time of entering the Proverse Poetry Prize competition, residing in Long Island, New York, where she works as a Marketing Assistant for a Biotech company. She earned her Bachelor's degree in Writing and Rhetoric at Salisbury University and hopes to continue her journey as a writer beyond the classroom. This poem is a stereoscope piece—it can be read paragraph by paragraph or line by line—and was part of her junior year portfolio.

RONY NAIR says that he has been a worshiper at the altar of prose and poetry for almost as long as he could think. They have been the shadows of his life.

Rony's work has previously appeared in or been accepted by *Chiron Review*, *Semaphore*, *Mindless Muse*, *Yellow Chair Review*, *Quail Bell Magazine*, *Ogazine*, *Two Words For*, *New Asian Writing*, *Yellow Press Review*, *YGDRASIL* journal, *Sonic Boom*, 1947, and others. He was a columnist with the *Indian Express*. At the time of writing, he is about to hold his first major photographic exhibition. Rony has been profiled by and has written for the *Economic Times* of Delhi. He cites V.S Naipaul, A.J. Cronin, Patrick Hamilton, Alan Sillitoe, John Braine and Nevil Shute in addition to FS Fitzgerald as influences on his life; and Philip Larkin, Dom Moraes and Ted Hughes as his personal poetry idols. Larkin's collected poems would be the one book he would like to die with. When the poems perish...so will the thoughts!

PAATA NATSVLISHVILI was born on 16 October 1952 in Tbilisi Georgia. He is the author of numerous books of poetry and essays in different languages and Professor of Media Communications at Grigol Robakidze University, Tbilisi, Georgia.

FLORENCE NG lives and works as a freelance editor and writer in Hong Kong. She is now working on her first collection of English poems.

KEITH NUNES lives beside Lake Rotoma, New Zealand. His poetry and short fiction have been published globally; he has been anthologised, placed in competitions (published in the 2016 *Proverse Poetry Prize Anthology*) and is a Pushcart Prize nominee. His book of poetry/short fiction, is entitled, "catching a ride on a paradox".

JUN PAN is an interpreter, translator and researcher and an interpreter and translator trainer. With a passion for reading and writing, she founded a Chinese poetry club and published a couple of Chinese poems (*shi* and *ci*) at the age of twelve at her birthplace in Xiangtan, Hunan. She then studied English language and literature in Jiangsu and interpreting in Shanghai. She came to Hong Kong in 2008 to study for a PhD in interpretation studies and has been teaching interpreting and translation at local tertiary institutions since then.

Jun has worked as an interpreter (and translator) for many years, although her childhood dream was to become a writer, director or painter. She has found her childhood immersion in Chinese classical literature and culture important and invaluable in her life and career. Apart from introducing Chinese culture to many of her clients when she worked as an interpreter, Jun also participated in the translation of several classic works from English to Chinese, including John Ruskin's five-volumed *Modern Painters*, Lyman Frank Baum's *The Wonderful Wizard of Oz* and *The Marvelous Land of Oz*.

Jun is now Assistant Professor in the Translation Programme and Director of the M.A. Programme in Translation and Bilingual Communication at Hong Kong Baptist University. She has also been playing the *guqin* (a Chinese seven-stringed zither) during the past seven years, which, she says, helps her to find an inner peace in her constant struggle and search for a balance between an oriental and occidental cultural identity.

LAURA POTTS is twenty-one years old and lives in West Yorkshire. She has twice been named a London Foyle Young Poet of the Year and Young Writer. In 2013 she became an Arts Council Northern Voices poet and Lieder Poet at the University of Leeds. Her poems have appeared in *Seamus Heaney's Agenda*, *Poetry Salzburg Review* and *The Interpreter's House*. Having studied at The University of Cape Town and worked at The Dylan Thomas Birthplace in Swansea, Laura has recently become Agenda's Young TS Eliot Poet and been shortlisted for a Charter-Oak Award for Best Historical Fiction in Colorado. This year, Laura became one of The Poetry Business' New Poets and a BBC New Voice for 2017.

CLAUDIA POZZANA is Associate Professor of Chinese Language and Literature at Bologna University. She has translated many anthologies of Contemporary Chinese Poets and has worked on the singularity of intellectuality in Twentieth Century China. She is at present working on the poetry of Chinese Migrant Workers.

JOANNA RADWAŃSKA-WILLIAMS was born in Warsaw, Poland, and spent a part of her childhood in London, England. She received her B.A. with a double major in English and Linguistics (awarded with Highest Honors, 1981) and her Ph.D. in Linguistics (1989) from the University of North Carolina at Chapel Hill. Her dissertation was published as *Paradigms Lost: The Linguistic Theory of Mikołaj Kruszewski* (Amsterdam: John Benjamins, 1993). Her research interests include the history of linguistics, language teaching methodology, poetics, semiotics, inter-cultural communication, and inter-disciplinary applications of linguistics, and she has authored or co-authored over forty journal articles and book chapters in these fields.

She is currently the General Editor of *Intercultural Communication Studies*, the official journal of the International Association for Intercultural Communication Studies.

Joanna taught Slavic Linguistics at the State University of New York at Stony Brook (1989-1994) and the University of Illinois at Chicago (1994-1995); and she has taught English Linguistics at Nanjing University (1996-1999) and the Chinese University of Hong Kong (1999-2003).

In 2003, she joined Macao Polytechnic Institute, where she has served as a Professor of English in the School of Business, the School of Languages and Translation and the MPI-Bell Centre of English.

Joanna's poetry has been anthologized in several collections, including *Lingua Franca: An Anthology of Poetry by Linguists* (edited by Donna Jo Napoli and Emily Norwood Rando; Lake Bluff, Illinois: Jupiter Press, 1989), *Montage of Life* (Owings Mills, Maryland: The National Library of Poetry, 1998) and *I Roll the Dice: Contemporary Macao Poetry* (edited by Christopher Kit Kelen and Agnes Vong; Macao: Association of Stories in Macao, 2008).

KERRY RAWLINSON gravitated from Zambia to Canada decades ago. She has won fiction, poetry and art contests (e.g. Geist; Postcards, Poems&Prose; FusionArt); has been a finalist in a few more (e.g. Mississippi Valley; Ascent Aspirations); and has recently been featured, for example, in *Pedestal*, *ReflexFiction*; *AntiHeroinChic*; *pioneertown*; *Centrifugal Eye*; *MinolaReview*; *CanadianLiterature*; *AdHoc Fiction*; *AdirondackReview* and *FiveOnTheFifth*.

M. ANN REED is a contemplative scholar, poet, Chinese calligrapher-brush painter and professor of English Literature and Theory of Knowledge. Her postdoctoral research studies the mending arts of Early Modern English and Contemporary Poetry. Her Chinese calligraphy and brush paintings have been exhibited in Portland, Oregon and at the Shenzhen Fine Arts Museum in China. Her poems have been published in various literary journals.

ANGELO RIZZI was born in Sant'Angelo Lodigiano, Italy in 1956. His mother tongue is Italian, but he is a polyglot poet, writing in Italian, Spanish, and Arabic. He has already published twelve collections of poems.

He has received many literary awards, including the following: Absolute Winner of, "Nosside Mondial Prize of Poetry", Reggio Calabria (Italy) 2004; First Prize (2008), Second Prize (2005, 2006, 2007) in the International Prize, "Tra le parole e l'infinito", Caivano (Italy); International Mention in the, "Alpas XXI Prize", Porto Alegre (Brazil), 2009; First prize at, "Città di Sassari", Sassari (Italy) 2010; Second prize for the poetry book, *Silvia o la ilusión del amor*, Jury High School in Sassari 2011; "Best Work in a Foreign Language", for the poetry collection, *Poésies depuis la ville de Menton*, at "Locanda del Doge Prize", Rovigo (Italy) 2013; First Award for poetry in a foreign language in the prize competition, "Città di Voghera", Voghera (Italy) 2014; Second Award for the poetry book, *Muhît al-Kalimât—Oceano di parole,* in the, "Il Litorale" Prize, Massa (Italy). Rizzi has also received two Critics' Awards and many Honourable Mentions and Special Mentions. He has been a Finalist in Italy, Spain, Switzerland, Venezuela, Argentina, U.S.A.

In 2006, he attended the UNESCO Congress, "Dialogue among the Nations".

He has participated in international poetry meetings in Rome (Italy), Havana (Cuba), Paris (France), Curtea de Argeş (Romanía), Djerba (Tunisia).

In 2016, the Academia Internacional de Ciéncias, Létras and Art ALPAS XXI in Porto Alegre, Brazil, nominated him International Correspondent Academic.

Rizzi is a member of REMES (Red Mundial de Escritores en Español); World Poets Society; Poetas del Mundo and SELAE (Sociedad de Escritores Latino-Americanos y Europeos).

His poems have appeared in anthologies and magazines in Italy, the United States, Switzerland, Cuba, Argentina, Kuwait, Brazil, Romania, and Hong Kong.

He has published the following collections of poems:
- *'Asfâr wa sirâb—Viaggi e miraggi* (bilingual) (Travels and mirages), ed. I Fiori di Campo, 2003.
- *'Inni qarartu 'Akhîran an 'arhala b'aîdan m'a-l-laqâliq—Ho deciso finalmente... andrò via con le cicogne...* (bilingual) (I finally decided... I'll go away with the storks...), Collezione Maestrale, 2005.
- *Decidí finalmente... irme con las cigüeñas...* (Spanish), (I finally decided... I'll go away with the storks...) Associazione Dreams, 2005.
- *Poésies depuis la ville de Menton—Poésias desde la ciudad de Menton*, (bilingual) (Poems from the city of Menton)**,** ed. Edilivre, 2008; ed. BOD, 2016.
- *Silvia o la ilusión del amor* (Spanish) (Silvia or the illusion of love), ed. Lampi di Stampa, 2010.
- *Tierra del Fuego* (Spanish), ed. Lampi di Stampa, 2014.
- *Il caimano* (Italian) (The caiman), ed. BoD, 2014.
- *Muhît al-kalimât—Oceano di parole* (bilingual) (Ocean of words), ed. BoD, 2014.
- *Guardando altrove* (Italian) (Looking away), ed. BoD, 2016.
- *Poesia della Nuova Era Vol. I* (Italian) (Poems from New Age Vol. I), ed. BoD, 2016.
- *Rotta per l'India* (Italian) (Route to India), ed. BoD, 2016.
- *El marcalibros* (Spanish) (The bookmark), ed. BoD, 2017.
- *Rosso di Marte* (Italian) (Red of Mars), ed. BoD, 2017.

JOSE MANUEL SEVILLA was born in Barcelona in 1959 and is a History graduate.

His first poetry book, *From the limits of Paradise*, was published in 1991. He founded "Poets against Aids" in Spain. He met his wife Julie Bisaillon on a plane. With her and Daniel Mateu and Guinot he founded the theatre Group "Bonobos"; they made people laugh and cry and had lovely nights together. After a trip to Croatia during the last European war, he wrote *The Bridge*, first staged in 2000 in Barcelona and in 2011 in Hong Kong, directed by Adam Harris. In 2004 he published, *Alice in Ikea's catalogue* (poetry), and had a photography exhibition, "Street Language", at the Hong Kong Festival Fringe Club. In 2009, his, *Ashes of Auschwitz and Eighteen Dogs*, was awarded the A. Urrutia poetry prize. And in 2012, his poem, 'Sonia Wants to Rent an Apartment', won first prize in the *Asian Cha* poetry contest, "Encountering". In 2016, his *Kennedy* was staged in Hong Kong, also directed by Adam Harris, and his poetry book, *Family Album,* was published in Madrid.

ALLEGRA JOSTAD SILBERSTEIN grew up on a farm in Wisconsin but has lived in California since 1963. Her love of poetry began as a child when her mother used to recite poems as she worked. Now that she is retired there is more time for singing and dancing as well as poetry. She has three chapbooks of poetry. In the spring of 2015, Cold River Press published her first book and she is widely published in journals such as *Blue Unicorn*, *California Quarterly*, *Iodine Poetry* and *Poetry Now*. In March 2010 she was honoured to become the first Poet Laureate for the city of Davis, California.

HAYLEY ANN SOLOMON is an author, librarian and poet. She is published in multiple genres, from poetry to historical romance, from literary short stories to fantasy. She holds a Master of Arts degree in Library and Information Science and once upon a time, worked as an academic librarian for the University of Otago, Dunedin. Mother and wife, she indulges her creativity with singing, chocolate and vibrant pink hair. She lives on the south island of New Zealand. and won a Supplementary prize in the 2006 International Proverse Prize competition for an unpublished manuscript. She also won a place in the inaugural Proverse Poetry Prize Anthology.

LAURA SOLOMON has a 2.1 in English Literature (Victoria University, 1997) and a Masters degree in Computer Science (University of London, 2003).

Her books include *Black Light*, *Nothing Lasting*, *Alternative Medicine*, *An Imitation of Life*, *Instant Messages*, *Vera Magpie*, *Hilary and David*, *In Vitro*, *The Shingle Bar Sea Monster and Other Stories*, *University Days*, *Freda Kahlo's Cry* and *Brain Graft*.

She has won prizes in the Bridport, Edwin Morgan, Ware Poets, Willesden Herald, Mere Literary Festival, and Essex Poetry Festival competitions.

She was short-listed for the 2009 Virginia Prize and the 2014 International Rubery Award and won the 2009 Proverse Prize. She has had work accepted in the *Edinburgh Review* and W*asafiri* (United Kingdom), *Takahe* and *Landfall* (New Zealand). She has judged the Sentinel Quarterly Short Story Competition.

Her play *The Dummy Bride* was part of the 1996 Wellington Fringe Festival and her play, *Sprout*, was part of the 2005 Edinburgh Fringe Festival.

DONG SUN is a Professor at Nanjing University of Finance and Economics, poet and literary critic, has published an academic monograph, a poetry book, and over a hundred poems in various literary magazines in China and many other countries. Her poems have been translated into English, French, Romanian, Turkish and Indian, etc.

ABBIE JOHNSON TAYLOR is the author of a novel, two poetry collections, and a memoir. Her work has appeared in *Avocet* and *Magnets and Ladders*. She lives in Sheridan, Wyoming.

LUISA TERNAU was born in Trieste, Italy. Since her childhood she has loved reading poetry from different parts of the world. To know more about the world outside her hometown, she has lived in several countries before coming to Hong Kong, where she currently calls home. Her first poem was inspired by observing her native town in the distance in the night time.

EDWARD TIESSE was born and raised in Washington State. When he was a teenager, he discovered T.S. Elliot, W.B. Yeats and the Beat Poets. Thus began his life-long love of poetry. He was an English major who taught for a while, worked in the restaurant business where he trained chefs, and, after graduate school, he worked for thirty years as an organization development consultant for a large aerospace firm. Although his corporate job kept him fully occupied, he always found time to write poetry.

Edward has many interests. He loves to cook and recently began baking bread which he soon learned is much like writing poetry. That is, the combinations of flour, water and yeast have many variables, and so baking is much like trying to find the right word and its place in a line. Edward also reads contemporary literature and travels extensively.

ROGER UREN is a former Australian diplomat who has also worked extensively in Asia, including in the Chinese media world, and written a number of books, including about Chinese culture and politics, and a slim volume of poetry. After working in Hong Kong for thirteen years and feeling relaxed by the Hong Kong tax rate, he realised the devilish role that tax offices could impose after he returned to Australia and spent more than six months there every year.

DEEPA VANJANI is Head of the English Department in PMB Gujarati Science College, Indore. She has worked as a freelance columnist for the local supplements of both the *Hindustan Times* and *Times of India*, also having published features in *Confluence*, a magazine published from the U.K. For the past two decades, she has taught M.Phil. English

Literature students at University and she is a registered Ph.D. guide of DAVV, Indore. Her first poetry collection, *Shifting Sands* (2016), was published by Proverse Hong Kong. In 2005 she won first prize in the All India Essay Writing Competition organised by the Association of Indian Diplomats, New Delhi on the topic, "India's Human Rights: India's Achilles Heel''. She runs a literary group named, "Shabd Shilp", to promote reading and writing activities. On International Women's Day 2017, the group published an anthology of short fiction (including one by Deepa) through Voice Verso, available on Kindle. She has also published research papers and articles in journals and books, and presented papers in conferences and seminars. She has been invited as keynote speaker, resource person, judge in conferences, workshops, academic programmes and literary events.

JOYCE WALKER is a retired administrator who has had poetry and stories published in a number of magazines. She won first prize in the Writers Brew story competition in 2002 and was runner up in the Erewash Writers Burst Flash fiction competition in 2013. Most recently she won first prize in the Writers Forum Poetry competition in the July 2016 issue of Writers Forum. She loves the First World War Poets.

BRUCE ARLEN WASSERMAN assembled his first poetry manuscript at the age of seventeen and later farmed and worked as a blacksmith in his twenties. He has received a B.A. in Mass Communications, a D.D.S. from the University of the Pacific School of Dentistry and a MFA from Vermont College of Fine Arts. In 2016, he was nominated for a Pushcart Prize. He is a book critic for the *New York Journal of Books* and the *Washington Independent Review of Books* and a Graduate Assistant at Vermont College of Fine Arts. At other times, he creates visual art as a potter, performs as a musician in a band, trains horses on occasion and is a dentist in clinical practice.

ELIZABETH WONG, popularly known as, "Libby", studied English at the University of Hong Kong, under the tutelage of Professor Edmund Charles Blunden, then Head of the English Department and British Poet Laureate. She graduated with a B.A. Hons. Degree, followed by a post-graduate diploma with distinction in Education. She also attended sponsored courses in New Zealand and at the Harvard Business School, USA, respectively.

A registered teacher in Hong Kong, she taught English before pursuing a career in the Administrative Service of the Hong Kong Government, serving in various key positions, including the following.

In the early 1980s, as Music Administrator, she promoted music and the performing arts and was instrumental in setting up the Academy for the Performing Arts (APA) in Hong Kong.

In 1987, as Director of the Social Welfare Department, she introduced major reforms, including the introduction of the Senior Citizens Card.

In 1990, she was appointed Secretary for Health and Welfare and was responsible for setting up the Hospital Authority (HA) in Hong Kong.

In 1995, she took early retirement from the civil service to go into politics. She was elected with the highest number of votes to Hong Kong's last Legislative Council under British rule in 1995.

In 1997, she quit politics to write. She has published novels, plays, poems and short stories. She has also worked with Hong Kong students on drama, poetry and creative writing.

She was a columnist with *Ming Pao* ('English with Celebrity') and *The South China Morning Post* ('On Second Thought').

For her services to Hong Kong, Her Majesty Queen Elizabeth II awarded her an Imperial Service Order in 1989 and appointed her a CBE in 1994. In 1995, she was made a JP and an Hon. Fellow of the Academy for the Performing Arts.

THOMAS YOUNG was fifty-seven years old at the time of entering for the Proverse Poetry Prize. He has been writing since he was thirteen. He is married, with three children and one grandchild. He never really thought about being published until recently.

SALLY YOUNGER is an award-winning author and science writer from Madison, Wisconsin, USA. Her first work of fiction was published in 2015 and received Great American Fiction honorable recognition.

THE EDITORS

GILLIAN BICKLEY, born and educated in the United Kingdom, has lived mostly in Hong Kong since 1970.

Her poetry collections include *For the Record and other Poems of Hong Kong, Moving House and other Poems from Hong Kong, Sightings, China Suite, Perceptions* and the bilingual English-Romanian *Poems/Poeme*. Two collections—*Moving House* and *For the Record*—have also been published in Chinese; individual poems have been published in Arabic, Catalan, Chinese, Czech, French, German, Romanian, Turkish and other languages. *Over the Years* (2017) is a selection from her previously published work, selected by Verner Bickley. In 2014, she was awarded the "Grand Prix Orient-Occident Des Arts" at the 18th International Festival, "Curtea de Argeş Poetry Nights", held in Romania. Gillian Bickley is one of the Hong Kong poets discussed in Agnes S. L. Lam's study, *Becoming poets: The Asian English Experience*.

Gillian has written or edited several non-fiction books in different fields: *The Golden Needle: The Biography of Frederick Stewart, 1836-1889 (founder of Hong Kong Government Education)*, Hong Kong Baptist University and David C. Lam Institute for East-West Studies, 1997; *Hong Kong Invaded! A '97 Nightmare*, University of Hong Kong Press, Hong Kong, 2001; *The Development of Education in Hong Kong, 1841-1897: as revealed through the Early Education Reports of the Hong Kong Government, 1848-1896*, Proverse Hong Kong, Hong Kong, 2002; *The Stewarts of Bourtreebush*, Centre for Scottish Studies, University of Aberdeen, Scotland, 2003; *A Magistrate's Court in 19th Century Hong Kong: Court in Time*, Proverse Hong Kong, first edition, 2005; second edition, 2009; *The Complete Court Cases of*

Magistrate Frederick Stewart, Proverse Hong Kong, 2008; *In Time of War* (in collaboration with Richard Collingwood-Selby), an edition based on the writings of Henry C.S. Collingwood-Selby (1898-1992), Lieutenant Commander in the Royal Navy, Proverse Hong Kong, 2013, *Through American Eyes: The Journals of George Washington (Farley) Heard (1837-1875)*, 2017.

Five of these fourteen English-language books received publication support from Hong Kong Arts Development Council (HKADC) and three from Lord Wilson Heritage Trust. The extensive research necessary for six of the non-fiction works listed was made possible by research grants awarded by the Hong Kong Baptist University and one was supported by a private sponsor.

Dr Bickley was Senior Lecturer / Associate Professor in the Department of English at the Hong Kong Baptist University for twenty-two years. She has been a full-time faculty member at the University of Lagos, Nigeria; the University of Auckland, New Zealand; and at the University of Hong Kong.

For several years, Gillian was an adjudicator at the world-famous Hong Kong Schools Music & Speech Association's annual Speech Festival and has also been a judge for the Budding Poets' Society Hong Kong.

More recently, as co-ordinator of literary activities for the English-Speaking Union Hong Kong, a non-profit registered educational charity, she has led reading appreciation sessions which are open to the community and assists to deliver reading courses at local schools. She has worked with the Gifted Education Section of the Education Bureau to encourage creative writing among students. On a freelance basis, she has completed teaching creative reading / writing courses at the Hong Kong Academy for Gifted Education (HKAGE) and at the University of Hong Kong School for Professional and Continuing Education (HKU SPACE) and been a guest lecturer on poetry at Lingnan University Community College. Her creative reading / writing course at HKU SPACE continues to be offered. In 2016, she managed twenty and hosted seventeen meet-the-author events at a Hong Kong bookshop.

Following her career in academia, Gillian has become an experienced publisher, project-manager, text editor, and production manager, including of poetry, non-fiction, fiction and academic writing.

She has been a member of the Society of Authors in the United Kingdom since her school days.

THE EDITORS

VERNER BICKLEY was born in the North-West of England, and educated there, in Wales and London, and has lived in Asian and Pacific countries for over fifty years.

He has been scholar, teacher, manager, broadcaster, stage and film actor and cultural diplomat in a life often enlivened by music and song, dance and entertainment.

Verner's many scholarly articles and book publications are mainly on educational and cross-cultural topics. He has however also published two volumes of memoirs: *Footfalls Echo in the Memory* and *Steps To Paradise And Beyond*. His five-book graded poetry anthology, *Poems to Enjoy*, has been popular since the 1960s. These now benefit from accompanying recordings of all poems in the texts (read mostly by himself, but some by his wife Gillian), as well as from teaching and performance notes. He is a member of the United Kingdom Society of Authors.

With his wife, Gillian, Verner Bickley is joint-publisher of Proverse Hong Kong and co-founder of the Proverse Prize and the Proverse Poetry Prize.

Verner was a naval officer in pre-independent Sri Lanka and India. He served in the Colonial Education Service in Singapore and, later, as a British Council officer in post-independence Burma, Indonesia and Japan. In Hawaii from 1971 to 1981, he served as the Director of the Culture Learning Institute at the East-West Center, established by the US Congress in Hawaii in 1960 and functioning as a US-based institution for public diplomacy with international governance, staffing, students and Fellows.

From 1972 to 1980, Verner led a small team of anthropologists, cross-cultural psychologists and linguists, focusing on the different ways in which individuals and whole societies cope in bicultural and multicultural contexts and how they address problems presented by different cultural norms. Among many interesting projects, his Institute provided for the pioneering voyage of the canoe, *Hōküle'a*, from Hawaii to Tahiti, disproving the theories of Thor Heyerdahl.

Verner was instrumental in bringing to conferences in Honolulu writers who included Guy Amirthanayagam, Leon Edel, Vincent Eri, Nissim Ezekial, Reuel Denney, Janet Frame, Allen Ginsberg, Syd Harrex, Thomas Keneally, Maxine Hong-Kingston, Arun Kolatkhar, Ananda Murthy, Kenzaburo Oe, Kushwant Singh, Kamala Markandaya, R.K. Narayan, A.K. Ramanajuan, E.R. Sarachchandra, Wole Soyinka and Albert Wendt.

After leaving Hawaii, and while in Saudia Arabia for a two-year assignment with the national airline, Saudia, Verner was responsible for a multi-national staff of 100 persons, mainly, but not exclusively, in Jeddah and Riyadh.

In 1983, Verner was appointed founding director of the Institute of Language in Education in Hong Kong and held that post until 1992.

Refusing to retire, Verner continues to live in Hong Kong where he writes and publishes on a variety of topics. He was founding Chairman of the English-Speaking Union (Hong Kong) and continued as Chairman of the Executive Committee for sixteen years. He recently passed this responsibility over to another person, but in his capacity as Chairman Emeritus continues with his own portfolio of tasks. As Chairman, he has traveled every year to the Mainland of China to join other judges of the national Public-Speaking Competition organised by national media. He has been an adjudicator for the Hong Kong Schools Music and Speech Association's annual Speech

Festival for many years and for a while was Representative in Hong Kong for Trinity College London.

Verner Bickley's experiences have created in him an interest in cross-cultural experiences and attitudes and in a desire to communicate what he has learnt. Through his memoirs as well as his personal contacts, he hopes not only to interest others, but to encourage them to build on their own desire to learn about and empathise with other cultures.

PROVERSE HONG KONG

Together, Gillian and Verner Bickley are the publishers of Proverse Hong Kong, a Hong Kong-based press which publishes both local and international authors, including non-native speakers of English. They are also co-founders of two annual international literary prizes for work submitted in English: in 2008, they founded the Proverse Prize for unpublished book-length fiction, non-fiction or poetry, and, in 2016, they established the Proverse Poetry Prize (for single poems which may have been previously published in a language other than English). In the case of both prizes, entries are received from around the world.

Beginning in 2007 up to December 2017, Proverse has managed, edited and published about 101 English-language books by Hong Kong and international writers, five Chinese-language books and one English / Chinese bilingual book. Of the English-language books, about nineteen have been awarded publication support by Hong Kong Arts Development Council (HKADC), one by Lord Wilson Heritage Trust and one by the Ride Fund for publication in the Royal Asiatic Society Hong Kong Studies series. One received a publication grant from the Ministry of Culture of the Czech Republic and one received a publication grant from the Ministry of Culture and Tourism of the Republic of Turkey.

Twice a year, Proverse organises literary events in Hong Kong, open to the public. New books are launched, writers are introduced and launching authors give brief talks. Announcements are made relating to the current year's Proverse Prize and Proverse Poetry Prize and prizes are presented to those authors who are present.

Gillian and Verner work hard to bring authors before the reading public. In 2016, they arranged twenty meet-the-author sessions, held at a Hong Kong bookshop. Edited videos of these talks are available on Youtube.

Of the titles published by Proverse, several have attracted a Preface or advance appreciation from figures of international reputation, most notably perhaps, from Václav Havel (for the English translation of Olga Walló's *Tightrope: A Bohemian Tale*).

Two titles (Peter Gregoire's, *Article 109* and *The Devil You Know*) were best sellers at Dymocks Hong Kong.

The publication by Proverse of the late Sophronia Liu's book, *A Shimmering Sea*, was a major argument in the award to Sophronia of a posthumous PhD at the University of Minnesota.

Other writers published by Proverse have also benefited in their literary careers.

Gillian's and Verner's books and all those by other authors published by Proverse, are available internationally as well as locally, including through the Chinese University of Hong Kong Press, and there are copies in the British Library and other legal deposit libraries in the United Kingdom.

POETS' NOTES AND COMMENTARIES

[1] Vinita Agrawal writes, "The Syrian conflict has been one of the worst humanitarian crises in world history with over eleven million people killed or displaced. I've been in empathy with the Syrian refugees since September 2016. For months news channels flooded my TV screens with images of lifeboats from Aleppo crammed with stricken people hoping to escape their war-torn country, setting out in the hope of building a future somewhere, anywhere, only to make it to poor accommodations in makeshift camps, yet thankful to foreign lands for giving them shelter, however temporary.

"I live in Mumbai so I didn't experience any of this firsthand, but the ache of a fundamentally human struggle—that of being forced to leave behind everything familiar, resonated with me deeply. It became an inkwell of emotions for penning the poem.

"My poem, 'Home Is Elsewhere', stems from that in-between land between imagination and real time coverage—where empathy takes the shape of very real pain. It is about evacuation and displacement mingled with positive aspirations of survival and rehabilitation.

"Home can sometimes be just a small fire, a roof that protects from rain, a nest where one can hold hands and express love. But for refugees, home becomes an exercise in self definition. When you're forced to flee everything you called your own, then the journey becomes gut wrenchingly emotional to say the least. My poem seeks to establish just that—that no matter where one lives, home in the real sense is in what has been left behind. Home is elsewhere."

[2] Indran Amirthanayagam writes, "The divide between innocence and experience has fascinated me since I first read Blake's *Songs* and Yeats's poems.
"I think that, 'The Lake Isle of Innisfree', is a perfect rendition of innocence while later in his life he confronts the truth in, 'Nineteen Hundred and Nineteen', of the weasel's twist, the weasel's tooth.

"My poem describes the journey from innocence to experience, from seeing the musical box in the shop window invoking the idyllic Innisfree to suffering the bomber on the high street, the cluster attack."

[3] Elena Maria Blanco writes, "The poem, 'Interknitted', reflects on the subtle emotional, psychological and practical transition from one object of desire to another, in which the passage of time is at once somehow (back)-stopped and exponentially accelerated as a powerful subjective force counters its objectively relentless flow. The subject's free will and determination, fuelled by love, assumes the fatality of time but makes it follow the lover's own design, symbolized by the knitting metaphor and the reprioritization of culinary and other habits for the sake of a new life model."

[4] Giorgio Bolla writes, "It's necessary to salvage memory. It can be found in visual dreams, taking the dreamer into strange closed valleys, where the light slowly ebbs away. Inside the valleys it makes sense.

"So, Poetry takes possession of her own tool—the Poet—and leads him to the vision of the road towards the divine.

"Thanks to Ione possessed by a god, Poetry runs without the weight of matter, in order to dominate the world of beauty. This is my Idea of Poetry.

"I picked her, and only her, when She arrived from the world of Ideas. Then the duty of the Poet is the proclamation of the freedom and the purity of the poetic action, beyond times and styles.

"Because Poetry means the time of recapitulation."

[5] Paola Caronni's poem, 'The Queer Eye', "has been inspired by the often difficult relationship between a mother and her teenage daughter. The 'queer' eye is the result of a physical as well as psychological reaction to the stress and worries caused by the tension and the distance inevitably growing between the two during the daughter's

adolescent years. The eye is also a metaphor of the mother's desire to see more than her sight can grasp, to go beyond the surface of the events and daily occurrences that happen to the daughter in a parallel dimension to which the mother is not privy. Sweet remembrances from the past emerge, of a time when the mother and daughter's eyes were still meeting.

"Khalil Gibran, in his poem 'On Children', writes: 'Your children are not your children'. My poem conveys the pain behind this reality."

[6] Benny Chia's poems in this collection, "are snippets of life real and imaginary; miasma from the Black Lagoon of the insomniac mind; bright and shine morning mental taichi exercises. All are as true as I know how to make them."

[7] Of her poem, 'New Sun', Psyche Chong writes, "One day, as a friend of mine was singing a story about himself, tears suddenly and silently came to my face. Mysteriously a scene of something like past life flashed through my mind and reminded me of someone I knew a very long time ago. The scene shocked me and wrenched my heart. The first two verses of my poem are a summary of his song."

[8] Teresa N. F. Chu writes that she grew up with dogs as family pets. Each dog brought its own story to enrich the family history, and to her, they are life coaches who loom large in her own biography, teaching her important lessons about living, about loving, and about life, and the inevitability of death.

She says, "The poem 'Adele' is dedicated to Adele, a tan-coloured mixed-breed canine adopted from the SPCA when she was just a few months old and who became the author's favourite 'child'. She was the author's strongest support in the darkest days of her life when anger filled her entire being, and she found herself breathing fire that always left a miserable trail of destruction and hurt within the family, with human and canine members all becoming fearful victims of this rage, rage triggered by situations and circumstances that entrapped her like Destiny. Adele, the bravest and the most devoted, chose always to stay by the poet's side, determined to sit through the roughest tempest and ride through the most dangerous storm with her, offering her body as a buoy to a master drowning in her own wrath. Despite the master's yelling and howling that must have been horridly magnified by a dog's heightened sense of hearing, Adele remained calm and quiescent, with not a cry or a yelp. Without this special guardian angel, anger would have consumed the author and there would have been no salvation.

"When the poet wrote this, Adele had recently passed away, put to sleep because of mouth cancer. It is the poet's wish that this sweet pet-pal princess of hers be immortalised, by a mortal's verse, which seeks to connect with her and to love her all over again, across the universe, across space, across age."

[9] Teresa N. F. Chu writes that, as already mentioned, she grew up with dogs as family pets, and since childhood, has always looked upon them as part of the family, to play with, laugh with, talk to, and to love and care for, till their departure from this earth whenever God should call upon them and lead them to the rainbow bridge, where all earthly pains will be superseded by divine pleasure.

She continues, "Sogaret, Michael, Cindy, Mimi, Dong Dong, Maggie, Toby and Adele (and still living with the poet now, Hazel and Hughie), each dog has brought its own unique story to enrich the family history. To the author, they have all been her life coaches who loom large in her own biography, teaching her many important lessons about living, about loving, and about life, and inevitable death. Through her mother's interaction with the dogs in particular, she has learnt the true meaning of love, which is, above all, commitment and sacrifice, both practised on a daily basis. From loving her canine friends, the author has also learnt to love and respect all creatures big and small, from whom the tapestry of life is woven to attain its colour, beauty and glory."

She concludes, "The poem 'Our Sweet Adele' is regrettably not the best tapestry of words, but raw emotions seek not carpentry; they just need a sanctuary. Of all the beloved doggies past and present, Adele was the author's top favourite and Adele's death, at a time and a date scheduled following the family's heart-wrenching decision, has prompted a release of emotions in this linguistic sanctuary, before they flow and find strength in a literary estuary, known as Proverse."

[10] Lucy Duggan writes that her poem, 'Ovenproof', "Expresses my ambivalence about the expectation still placed on women to be homemakers, bread-bakers, caretakers. It is about a mother who bakes bread for her family every week." It is written from the perspective of her daughter, who has not learned the recipe. In some ways, the daughter would like to create perfect bread the way her mother does; at the same time, the daughter wants to avoid becoming immersed in the role of a wife and mother.

"Initially, the poem promises to explain the recipe, and seems to emphasise the mother's creativity: 'She wrote... She made...' But then, rather than telling the reader 'the way to make bread', the poem lets the image of the finished loaves disintegrate: the recipe is forgotten. The work of caring for others ('reproductive labour') is repetitive and always remains unfinished: the bread is eaten, more must be baked. Thus, the mother's creativity is always undermined by the disintegration of what she creates—and by the fact that it is not regarded as art, hung in a gallery or printed in a book."

Lucy Duggan continued: "'Ovenproof' is one of several poems I have written about the many senses of the word 'proof': here, the bread has to 'prove' before it is baked, but the dough seems to be 'ovenproof' and remains raw. Questions emerge: what does the mother 'prove' with her lifelong unpaid work caring for others? Is the daughter 'proof' against gendered expectations?"

[11] Peter Freckleton writes this about the origins of his poem, 'Zanzibar Love'. "One sleepless night, riffing on sensuous sounds like 'z', Zanzibar came to mind, and verses followed, a totally non-factual play on phonetics and imagery.

"A sketchy fictitious back story emerged that there was once a grim tyranny of warlords, which gradually transformed into a pleasure-loving society, as some charismatic women attracted devoted personal followers weary of constant pointless violence.

"Those women became leaders, replacing the old warlords whose warriors abandoned them for the much more inspiring queens."

Peter also provides the following notes :
- "Cinnabar" (line 5) evoked cinnamon and vivid red, but in fact is poisonous mercury sulphide.
- "Zabaglione" (line 6) has the right sound, and luckily is also an ethereal Italian dessert.
- "Xebecs" (line 13) are sailing-ships with exotic spelling and, once again, the 'z' sound.
- "Ocarina celestinas" (line 16, verse 5) are hand-cranked organs, chosen for the rhythm of the name."

[12] Of her poem, 'For Joe', Sandra Gibbons writes, "My friendship with Joe developed over a period of twelve months when we met for one hour most Sunday mornings. I instantly knew Joe was a special person but I could also see that he was shielding himself from the world. It was not until Joe had returned to the UK that the pieces of his puzzle connected. This poem is a tribute to an amazingly talented and kind young person who fights internally to be appreciated. In writing this poem, I wanted Joe to know that I, for one, had seen inside."

[13] Sandra Gibbons tells us that her poem, 'The Candle', "Although only recently completed, was conceived over forty years ago when I was nineteen and struggling to make sense of my mother's severe and destructive mood swings from an angel of light to a devil of darkness."

[14] Elzabeth Grobler tells us that, "The more I read and spoke to people on the topic of happiness, the more it became evident that the same pearls of wisdom were repeatedly being highlighted by different people. This inspired me to write the acrostic poem, 'Road To Happiness', as a sort of mini road map to happiness or 'cheat sheet' for the examination of life that hands out 'tests' first before any lessons. I hope my poem will serve its purpose and encourage mindfulness and inspire people gratefully to live each moment to its fullest, but most of all I hope my poem will bring others happiness!"

[15] Elizabeth Grobler wrote the poem 'Spirit of the Horse' for her son Alrik Victor Grobler, born 9 January 2015, the Year of the Horse in the Chinese Zodiac.

"I did a lot of reading and research on the characteristics of this Chinese Zodiac sign as well as what the horse symbolises across cultures. With 'Spirit of the Horse' I endeavoured to portray the personality traits associated with the horse symbol as well as describe the twelve gifts of the human life-cycle and the beauty and importance of each stage. When keeping in mind Erik Erikson's psychosocial developmental stages as well as the twelve stages of the human life-cycle, it became evident that various horse-related animals as well as mythical creatures and what they represented could serve as metaphors for the stages of human development and transformation.

"The seahorse is representative of the pre-birth stage that holds potential and serves as a symbol of patience, protection, perception, persistence and contentment. The ancient Greeks and Romans considered the seahorse a symbol of strength and power since it was associated with the sea-god Poseidon / Neptune.

"The foal is representative of birth, infancy and childhood stages and represents hope, optimism and vitality. It also symbolises new beginnings and new directions, playfulness, creativity, innovation, strong motivation and vigour.

"The young stallion is representative of the adolescent and early adulthood life stages and serves as a symbol of strong emotions, passion, masculine energy, devotion and stability. According to the Chinese zodiac it's a symbol of practicality, love and endurance. In Native American culture, the horse is a symbol of the grounded power of the earth combined with whispers of wisdom found in the spirit winds.

"The unicorn is representative of the mid-life, mature and late adulthood stages which entail contemplation, benevolence and altruism. The unicorn also represents the spirit of purity, innocence, peace, prosperity, and wisdom, and the insight to recognise and take advantage of infinite possibilities.

"Pegasus is representative of the final stage of death and dying. This stage entails appreciating the value of life and reminds us not to take life for granted, but rather to live each moment to its fullest. It is the symbol of a free spirit and immortal soul.

"It is my wish that the 'Spirit of the Horse' and all the beauty it symbolises will be present in the life of my son Alrik."

[16] Kate Hawkins explains that her poem, 'Distant Homes' was written in 2017 using the new poetry form known as *Twin Cinema*.' "Three poems with slight variations and meanings can be read in 'Distant Homes'; one on the left column, a second on the right and a third reading the full piece together as one poem. 'Distant Homes' is a reference to two children dealing with the loss of their respective first homes, Singapore and Hong Kong. The poems symbolize that although we may feel alone in our own emotions we must remember that there are always others going through something similar. We go through life's ups and downs together as a collective experience, like the third poem does, bringing two separate stories into one poem."

[17] Kate Hawkins' poem, 'The Past Is Disappearing' is one of the first poems she ever wrote, some twenty years ago,

when she was 10 or 11 years of age. "As a child there was a deep sense of sadness upon leaving Hong Kong and moving back to Australia, a sense of loss that I couldn't really understand. Everything I was used to and took as normal had changed and I missed Hong Kong dearly. This was long before I learnt the term for children of expats; 'Third Culture Kids (TCKs)', so this poem was honouring the pain of loss and the acceptance of my new home. I hope my poem helps others put into words their sense of loss and change and also to remember that no one can take away your memories."

[18] Viki Holmes writes, "Waking up, after a night's camping, looking out over the sea and into the dawn, can feel not just like a new day, but like entering a new world. I wanted to re-image a camping trip as a voyage into something extraordinary, which is always how it feels. This poem, 'When we were kings of our castle', looks out from over the rugged contours of the Tai Long Wan beach, Sai Kung, Hong Kong, to the sea, and to new possibilities."

[19] Margus Lattik's (Mathura's) poem, 'Through the Eye of a Robinson's Needle', was written, "On a visit to the Philippines, 'the land of seven thousand islands', way back in 2005 ... [It] reflects largely on the contrast between the country's large cities and its remote wild islands and islets. Staying on the island of Palawan, I did venture into some uninhabited places like Tartaran which is where this poem was actually written. It also stems from the experience of people who have retired, temporarily or permanently, to solitary islands or solitude in general and found relief there. It seems that in our era of abundant socializing we sometimes neglect our other kind of connection to a less tangible or larger reality beyond ourselves and then try to find it by superficially recreating the beauty that was there for us in the first place—the beauty of being that can never be exhausted."

In response to a question from the editors, who had found, to their surprise, that there is such a thing as a

Robinson's needle (in fact two things, one being a magnetic surveying instrument, which just might have been alluded to), Mathura replied that, certainly, he had no intention to refer to this but was simply making literary and biblical allusions.

[20] Susan Lavender's poem, 'The Dying Bride', contains two concurrent themes.

"The first theme is the devastating effect of climate-change and human exploitation of our planet, as exemplified by Venice, a city gradually sinking into the sea due to climate-change and insufficient human intervention. In visual form, Venice's plight was highlighted at the 2017 Venice Biennale by Lorenzo Quinn's sculpture, 'Support', consisting of two giant hands rising from the Canal Grande to support the historic Ca'Sagredo Hotel from falling into the water. At the same time these hands have a menacing appearance, illustrating the fact that human activity has the ability to save or destroy.

"The second underlying theme of the poem relies on the personification of the Sea and Venice as husband and wife. The poem reverses the traditional personification of the Sea as a submissive bride to Venice, her dominant sea-trading super-power husband, as portrayed in the ancient ceremony of the 'the Marriage of the Sea', dating back to around the year one thousand AD. Every year around Ascension Day, a ring is dropped into the Canal, to symbolize Venice's dominion over the Sea. In my poem the sea is characterised as an abusive husband, gradually destroying his frail bride, Venice, as she succumbs and sinks beneath him. In this way I have sought to show how things have come full circle during the last thousand odd years, while also highlighting the exploitation of children and young women who in some places are still being forced into inappropriate destructive marriages.

"So readers are reminded through the poem's two combined themes that human beings are still exploiting each other, in addition to their environment, even in this so-called 'smart' (though not yet enlightened) 21st century."

[21] Lee Ching Yin writes, "Having an adventure nowadays has become rare and difficult, nonetheless, it is worth setting aside strenuous work in order to pursue a different kind of happiness in life." She says that her poem, 'Anthem of Splendid AdventureS', sings the unsung benefits of seeing the unseen and knowing the unknown.

[22] Peter Ho Cheung Lee explains the origin of his poem, 'The Morning Call'. "The failure to arrive at work on time on a particular clumsy morning reminded me that my parents were no longer around to wake me up. Moving on to the next stage in life struck me with a splash. This poem grew from the subtle emotion generated from this with an implicit time-gap towards the end when the narrator, having entered a further stage in life, listens to the remaining echoes from his past."

[23] Leung Ching Ning tells us this about her poem, 'Sonnet of the Weird Sisters (*Macbeth*)': "It was a snap decision. I was attending one of those Peel Street Poetry Wednesday open mics when they announced the 'sonnet-off' competition and called for entries for their upcoming 'An Evening with the Bard' Shakespeare tribute event. Up until now, I still have no idea what pushed me to sign up immediately with the idea of writing about the witches in *Macbeth*. For some reason I didn't feel a second of regret after making that spontaneous decision. I only wanted to create something really original and somehow I managed to finish the poem within a week even though I had never written a sonnet before. Perhaps the witches whispered to me telepathically. Perhaps I have always been one of them. Oh no, don't burn me please!"

[24] Marta Markoska's poem, 'Spiced But Chilled', was written as one of many "in a row", with a prefix of eroticism, which will be included in her newest sensual-erotic poetry book".

[25] First-prize winner, Jack Mayer, explains how his poem, 'I Am A God To The Birds', came to be written.
"I live in Vermont, in the northern USA, where winters are bitterly cold with abundant snow and ice. It's a challenging six months for those birds that do not migrate. Like many other people, I set out bird feeders in the autumn with black oil sunflower seeds and cakes of suet, high caloric blocks of hard, white fat.

"The feeder hangs outside my dining-room window. Every day, I watch the birds as they visit the abundant food I provide, taking their turns. When seeds and suet run out, I refill the feeders. One day, while watching a nuthatch and a finch after a snowstorm, it occurred to me that the appearance and re-stocking of the feeder must seem like a miracle to these birds, who cannot possibly understand me or the role I play in their survival.

"I felt somewhat superior, a feeling of *noblesse oblige*, until I sheepishly acknowledged that I am the same, grateful, but unable to understand what a greater power or spirit does for me."

[26] Maya Mitova's poem, 'Capriccio For Seven Heavens', alludes to the story, 'Wild swans', by Hans Christian Andersen. Readers are encouraged to take a look at this story when reading her poem.

[27] Kait Moller says, "I wrote 'Flooding Home' when I was in college and still torn between where I truly belonged. I traveled from New York to Maryland to attend school and, although the distance wasn't that great, was so captivated by the change of scenery that I was forgetting what New York meant to me. I felt like I was torn between two places, two sets of friends, two relationships, and two homes. So, fittingly, it only makes sense that this poem can be read two different ways. One side represents my New York life and the other my Maryland. Each side talks about a lover, a home, and the feeling like maybe I don't belong anywhere at all. I mention things specific to each place; for example, se-port a popular restaurant in my hometown and the

Chesapeake Bay filled with a popular Maryland beverage. The poem can remain separate or it can coincide. Either way, the concept of 'home' was overwhelming at the time, flooding in from all different directions."

[28] Rony Nair writes, "The Juwairiya poems of which J-5 is one, were originally conceived as a series of sonnets to bookend and occupy my book of poems that centred around the elusive, fugitive, nature of reminiscence. There was no religious or dogmatic allusion, but there were strands held together by memory, by hope, by moments of despair. The poems attempt to make sense of a feeling of loss, of time and tide moving on; and of frantic attempts to cling onto physical and sensory memory. The J poems try to encapsulate and hold feelings captive, even as they are swept away by the fragility of logic, by the reinvention of the self by the other, and by the stupidity of cowardice.

"J5 falls somewhere in the middle of the subset. It talks of life left behind after the sitter at one end of a see-saw drifts off, leaving the 'left behind' clutching onto strings, smells, roundabouts, words, errors, images of sunlight, food-cans; holding on even while realizing that the fulcrum would swing when one goes away…and all that is left behind would be memory. All that remains is a fixed point in time. And that the poet is cared for only by the poet. The other participants in the play have of course selectively rendered themselves amnesiacs.

"'Each man kills the things he loves', said Oscar Wilde. This poem was not about 'killing' but an attempt at holding on to sensory strands of sanity, of balance. And capturing it all down. At least the words remain…nobody and nothing else, does!"

[29] Paata Natsvlishvili had the inspired idea of asking Helene Margaliti, the translator of his two poems appearing in this anthology, to send the backstories that we requested, writing, "I thought it would be more interesting to get in the translator's shoes and hear about her attitude towards these two pieces and my work in general. She would talk better

about the English versions so I asked her to write these backstories. It will be more appealing for the foreign readers and it will be closer to their possible thoughts and feelings."

Here is what the translator Helene Margaliti wrote, dated, Tbilisi, 2017, about Paata Natsvlishvili's poem, 'Memory':

"'His poem is shivering and trembling, just like the string of the bow after lancing the arrow', so writes the French poet Athanase Vantchev de Thracy about Paata Natsvlishvili's poetry. That was the sentence I remembered when I started translating 'Memory'. While reading these lines you feel them becoming alive, trembling, trying to escape but realizing that there is no way out.

"Each person can have a different understanding of each word. The author is saying goodbye to his first love and it looks like the process of realizing the reality. It is the vow of love and devotion, giving up and fighting, losing and winning at the same time. These emotions become even stronger by his style of writing which reminds you of a very hard mathematical problem—if you want to solve it, you have to solve its parts one by one. 'Memory' is not like the ones you can just read and leave. On the contrary, if you want to follow the author's thoughts, you have to read each line very carefully. Each word matters and each of them can change the whole meaning. This is what makes it so interesting and special.

"It also sounds like music. When you're reading it, you hear the staccato playing continuously in your head. The melody never stops. It reminds you of the song you're obsessed with. And it is a serenade for the obsessive feelings and unforgotten love.

"Fortunately or unfortunately, the poem was very close to the translator's feelings and it wasn't hard to keep the emotional background. Anyway, the answer is finally found:
'Even if I forget you…
'I can't ever forget you.'"

[30] Here is what the translator, Helene Margaliti, wrote, dated, Tbilisi, 2017' about Paata Natsvlishvili's poem, 'Snow':
"My story goes like this: I fell in love with 'Snow' even before I knew Paata Natsvlishvili. When he asked me to translate his piece of poetry, I collected all the emotions I'd ever felt and tried my best to make the readers feel the same. So, each word is written with the highest level of care and fear of your reactions.

"'Snow' is a part of a poetic octave "Ia". Ia is a woman's name. Writing this poem, the author was thinking about his love from university, while I was thinking about my love from school. He was thinking about Ia while I was thinking about George. He was coming as snow in his town while I was 'snowing' in mine. But we were feeling the same…

"Paata Natsvlishvili describes love in a very pure, delicate and tender way. Love comes as snow—"at three o'clock at night", quietly and imperceptibly. And as the snow can fill up the whole town, love can fill up the whole heart and body.

"As the famous French poet Athanase Vantchev de Thracy says, 'All the poems of Paata Natsvlishvili are marked with an unusual nostalgia. Natural phenomena become alive and divine in his work. It is an epopee of an intimate landscape of the soul'. That's how his landscape is: the snow with the footprints—just like the heart with the scars.

"In the end, with all the sadness and nostalgia, you find the warmth which leaves you in a very bittersweet mood:

"'Don't ask me who I am or what,
Early morning you'll meet me in the town.
I'll be marvelously warm
In the frightening freeze around.'"

[31] Keith Nunes explains the background to his poem, 'A Juncture in Japan', as follows: "Some years ago during a

ten-month backpacking trip through Asia and the Middle East I spent a few weeks hitchhiking in Japan.

"I met some lovely people and never waited long for a ride. Some families housed me for a time.

"My poem is centred on these wonderful visits.

"I also added fictional elements and relished using some words from the Japanese language.

"For the poem's narrator there is a cathartic sense about his visit to the Japanese family having accepted his intimate relationship with an unnamed woman is over.

"I feel that leaves the reader with a positive."

[32] Jun Pan begins her comments about her poem, 'Farewell, D!', with two quotations:

"Is there such a thing as supreme happiness in the world or isn't there? ... What to do, what to rely on, what to avoid, what to stick by, what to follow, what to leave alone, what to find happiness in, what to hate?"—Chuang Tzu, *Chuang Tzu: Basic Writings* (Translated by Burton Watson).

"The supreme happiness of life is the conviction that we are loved; loved for ourselves—say rather, loved in spite of ourselves." –Victor Hugo, *Les Misérables*

Jun continues: "Human emotions usually find the strangest way of mingling. Lost happiness often results in sadness; yet sadness constantly mirrors yesterday's happy moments.

"An early spring morning in 2015, I received the last message from Fred's email address. Anne, his wife, told me that, earlier that day, Fred had passed away. My memory of the rest of the day was grey, a breathless grey.

"I first met Fred in Shanghai in 2004, when he was Warden of Kings County, Nova Scotia, and I served as his interpreter. He called me his, 'dear daughter in China', and I regarded him as my, 'Canadian dad'. We kept on writing to each other, on birthdays, Christmas, etc., for eleven years. I received twenty-two birthday and Christmas gifts from Nova Scotia, each handpicked by Fred and Anne.

"We tried to visit each other but failed for various reasons. In December 2014, Fred told me he had been diagnosed with cancer and would travel with the whole family on a cruise trip for Christmas. He wished that I could join them.

"I finally had my Nova Scotia trip planned for the summer of 2015 but never got the chance to meet him again.

"I eventually arrived in Nova Scotia in August 2015, as planned. I think Fred must be happy to see me finally visiting where he was from."

[33] Laura Potts explains that, "The history of 'The Night That Robin Died' is grounded in sad university nights spent sitting in box-rooms in the winter cold. After the books and late-night bars, I would return to my student house to watch Robin Williams on repeat from the warmest corner of a cold floor. In those small hours alone with nothing but his laughing eyes, I found in Williams a warmth from the childhood I found so bright in him. I have often stated that, 'something about him will always be young' to me. I was shaken upon his death to find that a part of the world that gave such comfort and infant joy way past my girlhood was suddenly lost. 'The Night That Robin Died' remembers the evening I heard the news. The poem slyly makes reference to moments of Williams's career: just as the caged bird recalls the film, *The Birdcage*, 'doubting the fire' recalls another film, *Mrs Doubtfire*. Recurrent images of light also honour his daughter Zelda's eulogy that 'the world is forever a little darker' for her father's death."

[34] Claudia Pozzana explains that her poem, '21st February 2002' is dedicated to her sister. "The two sisters live and get older in countries which are very far apart. The face-to-face dialogue between the sisters is interrupted and yet it is kept alive by threads of conversation from the past, said or suspended sentences forming a 'spiderweb of the mind' where the familial union between sisters is kept alive by looking back.

35 Claudia Pozzana tells us that her poem, 'I Never Call Myself', is about the fact that we all call others, "you" in both the singular and plural form, but we never refer to ourselves in this way. The implication is that we do not even know what to call ourselves! There is an understated indecision about one's own self becoming another self. The question then is, "how should we name this becoming?"

36 Claudia Pozzana writes, "The Chinese character for peace is '安an'. The idea of peace is represented by the reassuring presence of a woman under a roof." Her poem, 'PEACE, 安AN', she says, "evokes the meaning of the Chinese character for 'peace', introducing it in a modern context." She feels that, "The idea that peace is granted by the presence of a woman at home is not so credible in this age. Peace is coveted and needs to be declared today, the same way war used to be."

37 Claudia Pozzana's poem, 'Return, Sun', is based on a pun. "The Italian word for litmus is 'tornasole', which literally means 'return, sun'. In fact we are like litmus paper. Everything which happens to us in the world of reality leaves its mark on us, on our life, especially so when we are in contact with pain."

She explains that, "The second stanza begins with the two Italian words for 'return' and 'sun', immediately translated into French. The French word composed by 'return' and 'sun' means 'girasole' in Italian, that is, 'sunflower', in English. When in touch with love we shine like a sunflower. Yet this kind of shining is compared to the summer songs of the cicada, an insect which notoriously has only a very short span of life in which to sing. The transience of this shining is further exemplified by the image of a tourist.

"The third stanza," Pozzana states, "evokes the absurdity of litmus paper. It changes colour, but at night it is not possible to distinguish colours. As a result, silence is interrupted, giving way to the invocation, asking for the return of the sun."

[38] Claudia Pozzana writes that, in her poem, 'Tear', "The powerful image of the patient's 'skinned' heart suggests that there is a way out of pain, there is something in silence which gives way even to humour. The 'tear' of the title refers to the patient's determination to tear pain, the same way he/she struggles to tear away the strait-jacket from his or her own body."

[39] Claudi Pozzana's poem, 'Theme: Missed Encounter', is based on a personal memory of the poet. The point made is that a specific circumstance affects all that happens afterwards in one's life. This is true also, if, thinking about the past, one realizes that many different lives have been lived, not only one.

[40] In her poem, 'They Have Left', Claudia Pozzana refers to the fact that a dear friend has left, with both her good and bad character traits. Other friends have gone too. They will not come back to see the beauty of her summer garden.

There is nostalgia for missed dear friends and relatives, and a determination to overcome sadness by opening up to a new era of life, with new friends and new subjective concerns.

[41] Claudia Pozzana makes the following comment about her, 'Two Rustled Up And Found Again Poems': "The scenery in the two poems is to be found in Saturnia, a popular spa resort in Tuscany, known since Roman times. Being mostly frequented in the winter time, nests remaining on barren branches are reassuring symbols of continuing life.

"In the second poem the old people are well fitted to this wintry landscape with their tired and almost grotesque expressions becoming mellow on receiving a smile."

[42] Joanna Radwańska-Williams wrote the poem, 'Aerial View of Kunlun Mountains' when flying from Guangzhou

to Urumqi with a group of colleagues and friends. "We were a delegation from Macao Polytechnic Institute flying to attend a conference on intercultural communication at our partner institution, Xinjiang Normal University. When we were above the Qinghai-Xinjiang border area, the sun started going down and beautifully illuminated the Kunlun Mountains, which separate the Tibetan Plateau from the Tarim Basin in Xinjiang. My friends were excitedly taking pictures. However, the first words of the poem popped into my mind, 'and the sun will go down golden', so I wrote this descriptive poem instead of taking a picture.

"The hills are 'zebra-coloured' because at the point of writing the poem, the light was still bright and intense and made sharp contrasts between the white of the snow and the dark, almost black colouring of those areas which were rocky ('granite' and 'basalt') or which lay in shadows ('darkened precipices'). Also, we were flying fast and the light was changing its angles before sunset, so the mountains seemed to be moving like a wild animal. The poem captures the point in time before the onset of sunset, and anticipates that the scene will soon vanish before our eyes, the light will first become soft and golden, then finally dark at night.

"In addition to the play of light, there is also a water element in the poem: the mountains are the place where rivers originate ('from the inception of their course'), from the melting snows and glaciers, first in small streams ('rills'), then gathering water into rivers which flow down to the valleys below. The Yurungkash (White Jade River) originates from the Kunlun Mountains and flows through the Khotan Oasis into the Taklamakan Desert."

[43] kerry rawlinson reminds us that, "An Aubade is a morning love song, in theory to warn lovers of approaching dawn, when they must separate." She continues, "But May in Canada is Springtime, and this Aubade interprets lovers of all kinds—animal, water, tree, human—separating to come out and play with a glorious Spring day. Because it's a song, I include a rhythm to the stanzas and inner rhymes,

making extensive use of the long sound, 'a', as in 'May'. Since Spring is the season of procreation, all throughout the poem I've alluded, with subtle, playful references, to sex and coupling."

[44] M. Ann Reed's, 'Echinacea Making Moonlight' reveals the surprises and discoveries that occur when one begins to revise a mistake or a work of art.

[45] M. Ann Reed explains that her poem, 'Fire Under Water' reveals how a Japanese maple engaged her to notice the strength of gentleness and to recognize, "that strength from gentleness emerges from the tree's most fragile hollow core through which sunlight may radiate."

[46] 'Following the Life Force', M. Ann Reed explains, "reveals my first experience painting from life and how a live peony transmitted to me all stages of 'her' plant-life as well as what Chinese call "wu wei", meaning "effortlessness". This peony was a profound teacher, showing me how our understanding of the environment is most vital."

[47] Angelo Rizzi writes, "Consistent with my approach to meditation and spirituality, without any particular beliefs, nor belonging to any school of thought, my poem 'Today' represents the summit of the positivity ever achieved in my poems, a sign of progression and evolution within. Already in the title we feel the consciousness of the present moment. I am a poet but not just a poet. I am a multiform artist who loves to play the guitar, to paint and take photographs. In this poem I announce the beginning of my day with music. I assert my favourite passion of writing. The reason why I stress the fact that I choose on this occasion to write in my mother tongue is because my poetic path has been a little against the current. Following my studies (a Bachelor's Degree in Language, Culture and Arabic Literature from the University of Bordeaux in France), I started writing poems in Arabic; then I moved to Spanish; and then I came to my

mother tongue, Italian. My continuing poetry is accompanied by a veiled, almost timid romance. The end of the poem is a thank you to the Universe, a feeling full of happiness, possibly ephemeral, but true and perfectly present."

[48] José Manuel Sevilla has explained some of the background to his poem, 'Silence is not sad', as follows: "The Catholic Religion was compulsory in schools in Franco's Spain. The books for Primary school students were full of cartoons. The image of a boy free of sin was always of a fair-haired, clean young man with stainless clothes -- you could smell his mummy's eau-de-cologne on him. An Aryan. The image of a sinner was of a dirty, angry-faced and rather tall boy with, messy brown hair. He was dark-skinned. Obviously.

[49] Asked to explain to readers who the "Walter White" referred to in his poem, 'Soul Cleaning', is, José Manuel Sevilla writes, "Walter White—also known by his clandestine pseudonym "Heisenberg"—is the leading character in the multi-awarded American TV series *Breaking Bad*, played by Bryan Cranston. Mr. White is a talented chemist and a teacher who spends his life in a grey position in a secondary school. A loving family man, he is diagnosed with terminal lung cancer. To save his family financially, he goes into partnership with one of his pupils—a minor street dealer—to produce the best quality methamphetamine, which he is able to do thanks to his knowledge of Chemistry. An amazing resurrection, in Albuquerque, of Dr Jekyll and Mr Hyde.

[50] José Manuel Sevilla explains that, "Rome does not pay traitors", is a common saying in Spanish. "Legend says that the Romans had to fight a pro-independence movement in Hispania. Consul Scipio plotted with three of its members, close to the rebel leader, Viriathus, to betray and kill him. When the three came to claim their reward, Scipio replied,

'Rome does not pay traitors', prioritising ethics over the fact that their action had been initiated by him."

[51] For more than twenty years Allegra Silberstein has gone to a Tuesday night poetry workshop in Sacramento, led by Danyen Powell. "We bring in fifteen copies of our poem that we will read and then receive feedback from the other poets. The event in the poem really did happen one evening when I happened to glance up at a poet across the table from me. Our eyes met and were held as if in a magical time of love for a few moments. I know this poet well and cannot really explain that particular Tuesday evening.... that is why 'I ride the long shadows'."

[52] Hayley Ann Solomon explains that her inspiration for 'Happiness and I' came as a twofold happening. "Proverse was running a poetry competition on the subject of happiness, and there was an inordinate clamour among family and fans for more of my nonsense verse. While I write a lot of serious poetry, I am a veritable Dr. Seuss among friends. I was inspired to combine the topic—happiness—with the genre—nonsense verse—and see what happened.

"This is a nonsense rhyme, filled with the rollicking rhythms of youth, the swift pace denoting the playfulness of the metaphor. There is a certain stream of consciousness here, mirroring the bubbly, unfolding revelations of the meaning of happiness itself. The construct is that happiness is a friend, a teasing friend, but can also be irritatingly elusive, in the manner of hide-and-seek, unless its nature is recognized and quantified.

Paradoxically, in quantification, it will be found to be infinite, multiplying exponentially the more it is generously shared.

This is, of course, free form verse, with strong rhythms but no restrictive meter. There is a transition from whimsical to philosophical, with maintenance of the lightness of tone and, of course, a personification and ultimate dialogue with happiness itself. Rhyme is heavily used, but in a-traditional configurations to enhance buoyancy, reduce predictability and hopefully elicit laughter, a by-product, after all, of happiness itself.

[53] Hayley Ann Solomon's, 'Have I Found You, Utopia?', "was inspired by a recent discussion on the concepts of utopia and dystopia. It was argued that we are increasingly moving towards a dystopian world, and while this might be true in some respects, it led me to thinking positively about humanity and its achievements. In particular, I began to think affectionately of my own country, New Zealand, with its liberal emphasis on equality, literacy, and social responsibility. Before I knew it, this poem was born....

"The concept of utopia is generally discussed as an impossible ideal, an immutable dream that drifts into our consciousness then just as quickly drifts away, untouchable and unreachable. I have upended this notion, positing in my poem that utopia, certainly in New Zealand, is already extant.

"Utopia is not perfection, or 'heaven': rather, it is the parameter in which heaven can be forged. It is the ability to think and disagree without fear of repression and oppression. It is a manifestation of man's greatest strengths, his ability to use science and industrious activity to achieve monumental, almost miraculous feats.

"Utopia is the ability to appreciate the beauty of the world and the impetus to actually do so. It is the synthesis of opposites—as in the sashes of silk, representing aesthetics and ideology; and the sturdy apron representing hard labour and pragmatism.

"The poem could be described as prose-poetry: on the face of it, it is prose, but it is laced with metaphor and in particular sound play: assonance, consonance, half rhyme and echo. A rhetorical question is asked and indirectly, in the final dialogue of the piece, answered.

"Utopia is happiness, and yes, within the parameters laid out, it has been found."

[54] As both a reader and a writer Hayley Ann Solomon tends to dislike acrostics. "All too often," she says, "they are forced, trivial and rather simplistic. They are often constructed as phrases rather than sentences woven together semantically." She pondered this one day, wondering if it was possible to allay her prejudice against the form and write something that was both lyrical and meaningful within the prescribed constraints. "My inspiration," she writes, "was love, joy and music—universal inspirations, I suspect, but no less potent."

Her acrostic poem, 'How do I love you? An acrostic of Happiness', spells happiness vertically from the first letter of every line of the poem and concludes, both literally and figuratively, on the horizontal word, happiness. "The poem", she says "is a depiction of a true, deep love, with the implication that such a love is the equivalent, or progenitor, of happiness. Music has been chosen as the metaphorical medium because music is aesthetic, pervasive to the senses, sensuous, yet also, paradoxically, extremely mathematical and rational, just as the proper calculation of love would have to be. Love is grounded in both emotion and rational assessment of character.

"Whilst this poem is radically different in tenor and wistful lyricism than the other two poems that appear above it, it also uses sound play pervasively. As a poet, it would please me greatly to know the reader is tempted to read aloud, to hear the resonance and echoes embedded in the piece."

[55] Laura Solomon says that, 'Four Walls', was written while her flatmate, Sandeep, a Punjabi lady, was giving birth in the room next door. "Sandeep was a Polytech student and already pregnant when she moved into my house. Because she was foreign, a birth at the hospital would have cost thousands, I think nearly ten thousand dollars. Understandably, Sandeep did not want to pay this, so I said she could give birth at home, in my house. She organized it with the midwife.

"I was a little nervous about how the event would go and was not sure whether or not I wanted to be around for the birth. In the end, the birth took place at night and I was in the house. Sandeep began to breathe heavily as she went into labour and I was worried for her. I began to fuss and ask if I could get her anything. She said that no, she would be okay. She was very brave. In the end, the birth did not take too long, maybe only three or four hours. The midwife arrived with oxygen, which, as in the poem, was not used. The baby was born and was named Sanvir. He was very cute and we all loved him. Somewhere in the middle of all this action I wrote the poem 'Four Walls' Sandeep moved up to Auckland to find work; she was training as an accountant. I heard from her recently and she was doing well. The baby was taken to India to be raised by Sandeep's parents for the first two years of his life. Sandeep didn't feel she could work full-time and take care of a baby too, although she did have plans to retrieve the child and bring him back to New Zealand after his second birthday."

[56] A day care center recently opened next door to where Abbie Taylor lives. One day, she overheard one or two children admiring the tree-house in her back yard from afar. "The poem, 'Stay Away From MY Tree House', was inspired by one of those 'what if' moments I get as a writer. What if one of those kids sneaked into my yard, climbed my tree, then fell? What if I wasn't home, and the child lay injured on the ground for hours before help arrived? What if his parents sued me?"

[57] Luisa Ternau comments as follows on each of her four poems:

'Happiness on the Beach', "is a descriptive poem about a scene seen by the poet on a summer evening. Wild buffaloes often roam undisturbed among bathers on Pui O beach, Lantau Island, Hong Kong. It is rather rare to see them looking for food in bathers' bags though. The sense of happiness in the poem is implied by the silent agreement between buffalo and human. The former is craving some different type of food, the latter lets it go, and instead of turning the animal away, she laughingly starts filming the scene with her own mobile phone in order to share it and make it last."

Of, 'In Fear of Dusk', Luisa writes, "Dusk is when the sun light is over, when darkness arrives. It is a time to ponder over what has been done so far. Traditionally it is a time when working hours are finished and the rush hour begins. People return home, often dozing off or daydreaming, looking for potential shopping to do. In the meantime, life, exemplified by the heart image, continues, in spite of tiredness and a general feeling of unfulfillment. Life's romantic dreams are awoken. The dreamy mind imagines the presence of sleepy Cupid with his uncast arrow. The city lights cover the real darkness, belonging only to distant horizons. The city, like life itself, does not want to give importance to the dark side: life strives on in the chaos of pinging devices and artificial lights. Darkness is somewhat craved as it would mask the layers of dirt accumulated during the day, yet it is also avoided as something unknown and fearful."

Commenting on, 'Metropolitan Happiness', she writes, "The 'I' of the poem is meditating on their surroundings while sitting on an anonymous bench somewhere in a metropolis. Fast moving and colourful lights give the idea of life's vibrancy. Following the lights, the mind is transported to an imaginary sky where an angel steals the muser's idea of happiness suggesting perhaps that happiness itself is elusive, probably just a dream, something which is difficult to hold, even in the rich, stimulating and vivid world of a modern-day metropolis."

As for, 'Party Night', Luisa says, "Parties should be occasions for happiness. This poem is a brief meditation on the impact of a successful party in life. The poem suggests that, although parties are not part of daily routine, it is wrong to perceive the happiness they generate as separate from real life."

[58] Edward Tiesse writes that his two poems, 'The Jade Pagoda', and, 'Ha Noi Alley', were inspired by his travels in Viet Nam in 2014, "to visit our son and future daughter-in-law who live in Ho Chi Minh City. When visiting the Jade Pagoda, I was struck by the blending of religion, commerce and nature as well as the storied history of this pagoda. In our culture these facets are usually separate, but in Viet Nam they easily merge.

"In researching this trip, I learned of the interesting and colourful alleys of the major cities and was interested in touring them to learn how people really live. When we talked with our son about the alleys, he advised us against touring them because the alleys are peoples' living rooms and we might be invading their privacy. However, he did know of one that we should see and gave us guidance on being respectful. As we walked this alley, I found an openness in how lives were being lived and a nearly complete lack of privacy as their homes are exposed to those who walk by. The contrast between how these people live and how people live behind closed doors in the United States was stark."

Edward Tiesse adds the following note: "My wife Linda, who taught English for forty-two years, is my editor. I am deeply grateful for her guidance and insights."

[59] Roger Uren has always enjoyed satiric verse, because it is both entertaining and enlightening, and can express political views in a way that is not too cold or confrontational. Of his poem, 'Satan's Taxing Times', he writes, "This poem was prompted by my skepticism about the motivation of many governmental leaders around the world, who seem more interested in promoting themselves rather than making their own countries or the world a better place in which to live. So several years ago when I was filling out my Australian tax return I began to notice that much of what politicians were doing with the monies they gathered by means of

taxation did not in fact make their countries better, but, as it seemed to me, simply elevated their own personal status. I therefore began to suspect that they could all be agents of Satan, taking money from the pockets of ordinary people in order to advertise their power and importance. The result of this suspicion of how politics works is 'Satan's Taxing Times'."

[60] Deepa Vanjani explains that simple observations and pleasures have gone into making her poem 'Happiness Entries in My Diary'. "Most of these are drawn from calm moments spent during my visit to Hong Kong, as also at home. It is the simplest which are the greatest moments of joy. Days filled with the mundane, running-on-the-treadmill days, with no communion with nature, these are days which sap and drain me. These ideas have made up the poem."
She notes that the 'Peepul' is a sacred tree in India (botanical name, *Ficus Religiosa*), which, when it bursts into new life, has sprightly reddish-tinged leaves, which then turn green.

[61] Joyce Walker writes, "I'm now happily retired, but the inspiration for the poem, 'Being Lost Along The Way', came from all those days in the office when, for every piece of completed work, two or three more would arrive in the in tray, so that apart from the pay check at the end of the month everything seemed to be pointless as it was a never ending cycle.

"I'm sure I'm not the only person who's felt this way at some point in their lives and that other people can, therefore, identify with the sentiment behind it."

[62] Bruce Arlen Wasserman said this about his poem, 'Elegy For My Father'. "Perhaps the little things that interfere with our productivity in life are the things that are truly important. After my father's death, I found ample opportunity for reflection, both in a macroscopic way and through a close lens, about the nature of his life and his declining health. But the nature of death means there is no

longer opportunity to effect any kind of relationship change with the deceased.

"My poem, 'Elegy For My Father', provides a look at my own experience as my father's health declined and as that declining health exerted environmental change in his and my life. Through the poem, I recast what has been found through the benefit of hindsight: that every breath and each moment I had shared with my father was precious. That only impatience and indifference prevented me from seeing the value of those moments when my father was still alive.

"Through the poem, the essence of elegy is brought forth with all its intention, revealing the value of my father's life through my newly-opened eyes and sharing that elegy as a pivot for a reader's own introspection, perhaps becoming a focal point for changed perspective or an elastic anchor to an unknown thought that desires, more than anything, to become known."

[63] Libby Wong wrote this about her poem, 'Gratitude'. "As I turn eighty this year, I am more conscious than ever about mortality and the fragility of life. It has taken me eighty years to realize that the ability to be grateful makes me happy. I hope the recipient of my gratitude is happy too.

"I am grateful for every day that I am alive: that I still, 'live, move, and have my being' (Acts 17-28). I also realize that, at my age, the ability to say simple things like, 'hello, thank you', takes on a new glow, because these words come from the heart and these words say a lot.

"As we all know 'words' are powerful things. My thoughts flit to John 1-1 which says, 'In the beginning was the Word. The Word was with God. The Word was God.' Even though my word is not the same as 'the Word', it nevertheless lies in the shadow of the 'WORD'. My word is my bond and my feelings, expressed through the words I use, tell others who I am as a human being.

[64] Thomas Young's poem, 'An Angel's Kiss' was written for his cousin Melissa and her three year old son Brantley

who live on the farm next to his. Brantley was born in 2014, the day after Thomas's 55th birthday.

Thomas Young writes, "On 28 October 2016, Brantley was diagnosed with B-cell, Acute Lymphoblastic Leukemia. I wrote, 'An Angel's Kiss', during a particularly rough week of treatments last spring when the medication used to kill the cancer cells traveled to his brain, causing the white matter to swell. The brain injury caused many other side-effects and, of course a longer hospital stay.

"The poem hit me as I was pondering the things Melissa was going through and a Bible verse that I remember from when I was a child. That, 'we should not be forgetful to entertain strangers, for thereby some have entertained Angels unawares.' I hoped that writing this song would comfort and encourage them both.

"The original name of this poem is 'Brantley's Song'."

[65] Sally Younger tells us, 'Interlude' began life on a napkin at the Edgewater Hotel in Madison, Wisconsin, looking west across a wintering Lake Mendota.

ADVANCE RESPONSES

A look at the poems and the biographies impresses on us what *Mingled Voices* means: poets from all backgrounds and walks of life write in different styles and from different perspectives about happiness—or the lack of it. But they would all agree with Angelo Rizzi, who writes:

Today I choose my mother tongue
to put words
the one next to other
like roses in love.

Thus, poetry becomes the common denominator that plays an important role in every poet's life. There are two important things to be gleaned from this collection: happiness is often found in the small things and it is usually best understood in its loss.

Thanks to Proverse for giving us another wonderful collection of poetry that thrives on diversity—an apt reflection of today's world! To paraphrase Rony Nair, "when the poems perish...so will the thought", and so will happiness.

—**Birgit Bunzel Linder**,
    Author of the poetry collections
    Shadows in Deferment,
    (Winner of the Proverse Prize 2012),
    and *Bliss of Bewilderment* (Proverse, 2017)

In these times of tensions between countries and peoples, it is refreshing to see a multitude of poets from around the globe crossing borders with their words and attesting to our ultimate humanity from birth to death and beyond.

—**Agnes Lam,**
Author of four poetry collections, including
A pond in the sky (2013)
and *Poppies by the motorway* (CUHK Press, 2017)

Reading the poems in *Mingled Voices 2* is like going on a global journey. The poems are adventures into foreign landscapes, geographical and mental, whether seen through the eyes of a refugee, a transient visitor, or the child of an expat. But above all, the poems are about the human heart, and our constant search for home and happiness.

—**Lelawattee Manoo-Rahming**,
Author of the poetry collections,
    Curry Flavour (Peepal Tree Press, 2000)
    and *Immortelle and Bhandaaraa Poems,*
    (Inaugural Proverse Prize Finalist (2009)).

POETRY PUBLISHED BY PROVERSE

Astra and Sebastian, by L. W. Illsley

Bliss of Bewilderment, by Birgit Bunzel Linder. 2017.

Chasing Light, by Patricia Glinton Meicholas. 2013.

China Suite and other Poems, by Gillian Bickley. 2009.

For the Record and other Poems of Hong Kong, by Gillian Bickley, 2003.

Frida Kahlo's Cry and other Poems, by Laura Solomon. 2015.

Home, Away, Elsewhere, by Vaughan Rapatahana. 2011.

Immortelle and Bhandaaraa Poems, by Lelawattee Manoo-Rahming. 2011.

In Vitro, by Laura Solomon. 2nd ed. 2013.

Irreverent Poems for Pretentious People, by Henrik Hoeg. 2016.

Mingled Voices: The inaugural Proverse Poetry Prize Anthology (2016), edited by Gillian and Verner Bickley. 2017.

Moving House and other Poems from Hong Kong, by Gillian Bickley. 2005.

Of Symbols Misused, by Mary-Jane Newton. March 2011.

Over the Years, by Gillian Bickley. 2017.

Painting the Borrowed House: Poems,
by Kate Rogers. 2008.

Perceptions, by Gillian Bickley. 2012.

Rain on the Pacific Coast, by Elbert Siu Ping Lee. 2013.

refrain, by Jason S. Polley. 2010.

Shadow Play, by James Norcliffe. 2012.

Shadows in Deferment, by Birgit Bunzel Linder. 2013.

Shifting Sands, by Deepa Vanjani. 2016.

Sightings: a collection of poetry, with an essay, 'communicating poems', by Gillian Bickley. 2007.

Smoked pearl: Poems of Hong Kong and Beyond,
by Akin Jeje (Akinsola Olufemi Jeje). 2010.

The Burning Lake,
by Jonathan Locke Hart. November 2016.

Unlocking, by Mary-Jane Newton. 2013.

Wonder, Lust & Itchy feet, by Sally Dellow. 2011.

POETRY – CHINESE LANGUAGE

For the record and other poems of Hong Kong,
   by Gillian Bickley. Translated by Simon Chow. 2010.

Moving House and other poems from Hong Kong, translated into Chinese, with additional material,
   by Gillian Bickley.
   Edited by Tony Ming-Tak Yip.
   Translated by Tony Yip & others. 2008.

FIND OUT MORE ABOUT PROVERSE AUTHORS, BOOKS, EVENTS AND INTERNATIONAL PRIZES

Visit our website
http://www.proversepublishing.com
Visit our distributor's website
<www.chineseupress.com>

Follow us on Twitter
Follow news and conversation:
<twitter.com/Proversebooks>
OR
Copy and paste the following to your browser window and follow the instructions:
https://twitter.com/#!/ProverseBooks

"Like" us on www.facebook.com/ProversePress

Request our E-Newsletter
Send your request to info@proversepublishing.com.

Availability
Most titles are available in Hong Kong and world-wide from our Hong Kong-based Distributor,
The Chinese University Press of Hong Kong,
The Chinese University of Hong Kong, Shatin, NT, Hong Kong SAR, China. Web: chineseupress.com.
All titles are available from Proverse Hong Kong and the Proverse Hong Kong UK-based Distributor.
We have stock-holding retailers in Hong Kong, Singapore (Select Books),
Canada (Elizabeth Campbell Books),
Principality of Andorra (Llibreria La Puça, La Llibreria).
Orders can be made from bookshops in the UK and elsewhere.

Ebooks
Most of our titles are available also as Ebooks.

www.ingramcontent.com/pod-product-compliance
Lightning Source LLC
Chambersburg PA
CBHW051125160426
43195CB00014B/2342